Praise for *How to Survive the End of the World*

'A fast-paced, amusing and ░░░░░░░░░░░░░░░
anyone dealing w░░ ░░░░░░ problems'
Guardian

'One of the things that really marks Aaron's book out
from others on the market that tackle the topic of mental
health is that it's quite simply laugh-out-loud funny. He
manages to harness the ludicrous, the awkward, and the
downright bizarre things he's done because of mental
health issues, and turn them into hilarious anecdotes'
Independent

'A brilliant and funny read for the apocalyptically
minded . . . If you enjoy his stuff on the Twitter, you'll
love him minus a character limit'
Matt Haig, author of *Reasons to Stay Alive*

'In a sea of books about mental health, it stands out for
its humour, wisdom and lightness of touch'
Adam Kay, author of *This is Going to Hurt*

'I LOVED it because it's good to know that I'm not the
only one pretending everything's fine, even when
everything is fine'
Juno Dawson, author of *The Gender Games*

'It is excellent'
Dr Fern Riddell, author of *Death in Ten Minutes*

'A frantically hilarious and deeply insightful exploration of
life inside a brain that's constantly under siege from itself'
Dean Burnett, author of *The Idiot Brain*

How to Survive the End of the World (When It's in Your Own Head)

An Anxiety Survival Guide

AARON GILLIES

TWO ROADS

www.tworoadsbooks.com

First published in Great Britain in 2018 by Two Roads
An imprint of John Murray Press
An Hachette UK company

1

This paperback edition first published in 2019

A CIP catalogue record for this title
is available from the British Library

Paperback ISBN 9781473659711
eBook ISBN 9781473659728
Audio Digital Download ISBN 9781473660915

Typeset in Sabon by Palimpsest Book Production Limited,
Falkirk, Stirlingshire

Printed and bound in Great Britain by Clays Ltd, Elcograf S.p.A.

Hodder & Stoughton policy is to use papers that are natural,
renewable and recyclable products and made from wood
grown in sustainable forests. The logging and manufacturing
processes are expected to conform to the environmental
regulations of the country of origin.

Hodder & Stoughton Ltd
Carmelite House
50 Victoria Embankment
London EC4Y 0DZ

For anyone who has ever felt a little bit crazy

CONTENTS

0.5
PROLOGUE.

Wait, no.

DISCLAIMER.

Wait, no.

THE BEGINNING BIT OF THE BOOK BEFORE WE REALLY GET INTO STUFF, WHERE I JUST TALK SHIT FOR A BIT IF THAT'S OK.

Bollocking fucking shitting titting arsing hell, I'm having a panic attack. It feels like a cannonball has been surgically implanted into my lower intestine. My lungs are both full and empty at the same time because my breathing is so manic that I am now failing at the most basic of human functions. My entire chest feels like I'm

1

being crushed under the weight of a small family caravan. My arms are numb. I am paralysed by irrational terror. I honestly feel like I am about to die. No wait, I *am* about to die. I am going to leave this planet on a heaving Northern Line train somewhere between Angel and King's Cross. This situation is less than ideal.

Panic attacks. They are the human equivalent of your computer freezing because you asked it to do too many things at once. An overload of information has caused the whole system to go into meltdown. Now it's just doing the circle of doom, where the mouse doesn't work, you can't close any applications and some awful music (something really annoying, probably involving a sousaphone) plays in three-second loops in the background. The beautifully timed panic attack I described in the previous paragraph was the result of simply being on a busy train. After I have a panic attack, I try to evaluate it and identify what triggers were in place. This time, it was just that it was a bit busy. An overload of confusion, fear and worry caused my entire brain computer to freeze. And what was I doing on the train? Reading a book on how to handle social anxiety while on the way to collect my prescription of Citalopram (an anti-anxiety medication). I am so on brand.

I exited the train at the next station and sat on the nearest bench. I put my head in my hands and counted from one to four slowly in my head, attempting to wrangle my breath back into submission in time with the count. Ten minutes later I was ready and raring to go. I was back to being me.

After being diagnosed with severe anxiety, I read everything I could on the subject. Before my diagnosis I had – wrongfully – assumed that this was just the way everyone was. I thought that this was the way that all our brains are wired, that everything in the world was terrifying and we all lived with a shroud of fear covering every aspect of our lives. And then I went to the doctor's.

The doctor showed me a graph and said 'Most people are here' as he pressed his finger on the screen (never put your finger on the screen of a computer, that's disgusting) and pointed to a nice blue section of the bar graph. 'And you are here,' he said as he raised his index finger to the top of the graph, where everything was red and the word 'SEVERE' was in bold Comic Sans. My first thought was, 'I don't want my mental health determined by anything that uses the font Comic Sans.' I felt personally attacked; he might as well have told me that my brain is a mess while doing a sarcastic impression of me.* But as I walked out of his office, holding a piece of paper that said 'SEVERE', but this time in Times New Roman, I finally had something I could deal with. The thing in my brain had a name. I finally had an enemy I could fight, and my enemy's name was severe anxiety.

---

* I imagine a sarcastic impression of me to be someone waving a bottle of rum around and saying 'Oooo I have mental problems' in a high-pitched voice.

This is the part where I inform you that I am not a doctor, I am not a professionally trained mental health spokesperson – bloody hell, I'm barely a functioning adult most of the time. (All I ate yesterday was strawberry laces, because I am an adult.) The thing that allows me to write about this subject is that it has been a huge part of my life for quite some time now. You know how some people have one defining personality characteristic? Like Jane in Accounts who is obsessed with her cat, Mittens, or Brian from the gym who only ever speaks about the new diet he is on where he has to eat a raw egg every 29 seconds. It's like that, but my thing is anxiety. The super awesome fun thing about having anxiety is it's bloody hard to talk about it with any other human being because talking about yourself makes you anxious. But when I was diagnosed I started reading blogs and articles from people who seemed a lot more in tune with their anxiety. Their words and the sense of control they seemed to have over their disorder gave me hope, so I began writing too. Most of it I didn't post, because most of it was the drunken ramblings of a moron, but it started to help. A year after my diagnosis I found that talking and reading; these were the things that actually helped me. They put my condition into perspective, and gave it parameters I could understand and fight against.

Anxiety is a completely individualistic disorder: my experience will be different from yours, and yours will be different from the next person's, and so on. But even if we are all fighting our own unique battles, we can fight them together. We can normalise a condition that is still seen by many as a weakness, or a character flaw. Through conversation and education we can help ourselves and help others, because we are, quite frankly, fucking brilliant.

A theme I noticed in a lot of books on anxiety and mental health is that the writer will fall into the cliché of 'misery memoir'. It can be just 80,000 words about how bad they have it and then, wait, OK, everything is fine now. I want to avoid that. You don't want to know about me, I am boring. I put my Totoro* onesie on one leg at a time just like everyone else. I do, however, need to explain why *I* am writing this, and to give my condition a bit of context, so we will cram that into a different couple of chapters and we will never speak of it again. (I lie, I'll probably bring it up over and over again but don't worry too much, we will get through this.) Just regard these chapters as the literary equivalent of when your aunt comes round at Christmas, gets drunk, ruins the entire day, then leaves in blissful ignorance, though hopefully this book won't be as emotionally scarring. In the following nonsensical ramblings that have been collectively labelled a 'book', you'll find examples of my own experiences with anxiety, some fairly badly written metaphors, investigations and analyses, interviews with other people who

---

* If you don't know who Totoro is I suggest you put this book down, go watch the entire Studio Ghibli film collection and then come back so you'll get the reference.

suffer with anxiety and their unique experiences with the disorder, long sciencey words to make me sound clever and fairly terrible attempts at humour, because levity is the . . . something of something. To put it simply, let's find out how to survive anxiety, and let's kick its arse together.

1.
THE CLICHÉD INTRO

(AKA Me, Me, Me)

The human brain can do anything. It can compose symphonies, theorise on the vast absurdity of the cosmos, create artwork that can make grown humans cry. It can love, it can make connections with other human beings that can define your entire existence, it can relay experiences to others in prose and poetry. It can invent, innovate and pioneer. It's really quite incredible. But when I talk to my anxious brain about this, it's less than reasonable:

Anxious brain: **'Let's have anxiety!'**
Me: 'But, but the other things?!'
Anxious brain: **'You heard me.'**

You know that trope in movies where an angel and a devil appear on the protagonist's shoulders? Now imagine that, but it's just a boring, annoying, tiny version of yourself that appears on your shoulder to tell you everything that you're doing wrong with your life and revels in over-analysing everything you do. This version of yourself permanently rents the space on your shoulder and you can't evict it – it's claimed squatters' rights, it's a part of your day-to-day. And frankly, it is a massive fucking inconvenience.

But let's start somewhere that isn't bogged down in an overly laboured analogy. Let's start with the total bin fire that is my brain.

I'm mad. I know you shouldn't use the word 'mad' as an adjective to describe mental health disorders. It is, of course, a gross oversimplification and a term used flippantly by people who think 'random' is a personality trait. But it's easier to say to myself that I'm mad than to say, 'I have several quite prevalent mental health disorders that manifest in many bizarre ways and I am dealing with them extremely poorly through medication, self-pity and an often crass use of deflective humour.' Maybe let's not go with mad. Let's go with 'unique'. Or 'bananas'. Or 'straight up bonkers'. Basically I need a word that differentiates the nonsense that happens in my own mind from what goes on in everyone else's. I'm different. I am different to how I perceive everyone else in the world to be. I watch the other human beings, all of whom seem to have their shit together, doing their best in the world and I simply panic. I convince myself that I am losing my mind. My friends on Facebook post things about their marriages, their children, their brand new horse harpoons or whatever midlife-crisis shopping they are currently doing, and the closest I get to posting an interesting, life-affirming Facebook status is: 'I ate an entire share bag of crisps by myself today' or 'I managed to hold a conversation with another person for almost two and a half minutes today and I only wanted to run away sixty-three times.' With the benefit of having worked on my anxiety for years, I know this is just my brain over-analysing everything, I can have a tendency to judge myself by the achievements of others, when the truth here is that no one has their shit together. No one knows what they are doing; in every supposedly happy Facebook post there is realism, hidden behind a bad photo filter.

We are all winging it – some of us are just better at convincing ourselves than others. At school they imply that by the time you're thirty you'll have your entire life figured out. You'll have whatever fantastical job you dreamed about at the age of six, you'll have a picturesque family with beautiful children, a dog called Ruffles or Barry or something, a herb garden, disposable income and a secret alcohol dependency. In reality, every person, or at least 90% of us, at any stage of our being on this planet, is screaming internally and wondering what the fuck is going to go wrong next. I know this, I can accept this, but I panic, I feel like I slip further down a rabbit hole of my own invention. This is just how my brain is wired. I can't take it back under warranty and ask for a new one, or take it to a Genius

Bar and ask for a replacement part. The most I can do is try to understand why my brain programmed itself this way.

A BRIEF HISTORY OF MY BRAIN

Step one: Depression

Being a teenager is pretty much an awful experience for everyone. Your body hates you, so it makes everything as awkward as it possibly can – just in case social hierarchies weren't enough to worry about, now you have just one pube and a weirdly small testicle. You're completely obsessed with social status, education and expectation. Which means that any form of self-care can fall by the wayside. In retrospect I was depressed long before I was diagnosed but I didn't know what depression was when I was a teen. Depression was something my music heroes had, it wasn't for people who worked in petrol stations: you felt bad, you got on with it. Well that's what I thought, but what I didn't know was that if you hide something inside yourself for long enough, you break.

I was twenty-two when I first convinced myself to see a therapist.* The first question they asked was, 'How was your childhood?' It had taken me four years

---

* The events that led me to search for a therapist included a pirate costume, three bottles of rum and a Facebook post that makes the lyrics of a Radiohead song seem like a nursery rhyme.

to get to the stage where I thought I could handle therapy. It was the fourth time I had been referred by my doctor and every other time I had ignored it, or made excuses about how therapy wasn't for me. A master in the art of procrastination, I treated my mental illness like a sprained ankle. Ignorance was indeed bliss in this case. 'If I ignore it, it will just fix itself'/'These things sort themselves out, don't they?' SPOILER ALERT: these things do not 'sort themselves out'. In fact it takes a lot of hard work and perseverance to start to understand your own brain.

Imagine how much easier things would be if your brain had a manual. You could just flick to the index, go to M, find 'mental illness' and there would probably be a way you could turn it all off and back on again and hope for the best. Wait, I think turning your brain on and off again is technically dying and being reincarnated so ignore that metaphor. Or is it a coma? Let's skip this bit, I'm stuck in a loop.

Not to sound like Mr Obvious here, but the hardest part of any mental illness is coming to terms with it. Admitting that you need help, that you can't do this by yourself, that you are struggling with being you. You can try the pills, the mindfulness, the therapy, the yoga, the clean eating, changing your lifestyle – different things work for different people. So far I have found a mixture of medication and various Nic Cage movies from the 90s are the closest I get to mindfulness. The one thing I remember about sitting in the therapist's waiting room that day was that 'Don't Worry, Be Happy' by Bobby McFerrin started playing on the radio. All the other patients in the waiting room looked at each other with an expression of 'This is a fucking joke, right?' on their faces. I started laughing – my go-to response, my safety blanket. My first trip to the therapist was already like a poorly written sitcom.

'How was your childhood?' I thought therapists only asked that in movies just before the protagonist broke down in tears and started screaming 'ROSEBUD' or something. I wasn't ready for that question. I wanted to talk about the present me, the me that was fucking up my life right now. Like many sufferers I had come to the conclusion that I somehow deserved this. Maybe it was penance for leading a worthless life, maybe it was punishment for being a bad person in a previous life, maybe it was karma for that time I ate an apple while walking around the supermarket before paying for it. I don't believe in previous lives, but as I sat in the therapist's office, his questions going straight over my head, I seriously considered the idea that if this *was* karma kicking me in the unmentionables, then I must have been a complete bastard in my previous existence. Like Hitler's life coach, or Donald Trump's wig adviser or something. I sat and continued to contemplate this nonsense as the therapist stared at me in silence. I was wasting quite valuable time but I did have a major breakthrough, I think I figured out who previous me must have been – I am 99% sure previous me must have perished after inspiring the headline 'Local man thinks wooden horse is a completely innocent gift for city'.

Back when I started learning that my brain was against me, and that its favourite hobby was coming up with new fun mental health disorders for me to deal with, I handled it the way any early-twenties beta male would: I drank and ignored it. As a Brit, this is how I deal with many bad situations. Bad day? Glass of wine! Big bill comes through the post that we can't really afford at the moment? A couple of gin and tonics! A mental health disorder that you're not ready to battle right now? An entire bathtub filled with cheap rum, please! I could feel my sanity slipping further away every morning as I looked in the mirror and hated what was reflected back at me. The thing about ignoring something as damaging as mental health problems is that they don't dissipate, they simply get worse and worse. They rot you from the inside out until something forces you to acknowledge them. I'll skip the gory details here, but needless to say, I broke.* And that's when I admitted to myself that I wasn't normal.

Anyway, the childhood question.

I answered honestly. My childhood was good. My parents were great parents. My school was a good school. I had great friends. I went to school discos and danced with girls. I did the stupid things kids are

---

* There will be a section in a later chapter that goes into the dark side of mental health problems, and there will also be a trigger warning for that before it arrives, but for now I thought we'd keep it light and breezy. Well, not light and breezy, maybe just not massively heavy and gusty. Yeah.

supposed to do. My childhood was normal. It wasn't the cause of my internal bedlam. I became depressed when I was in my early teens, and was diagnosed in my early twenties.* I can't pinpoint the exact moment as it wasn't a case of a switch being thrown. 'Sane' didn't suddenly turn to 'mad as a box of frogs'. It was gradual, but I do remember being 'normal', and then I remember one day taking stock of my life and realising that I was no longer what I thought society defined as 'normal'. I drank to excess for no reason. I either slept for three days or didn't sleep for a week. I ate like a Hungry Hungry Hippo or forgot to eat for seventy-two hours. I was irrational. I was erratic. I wasn't me.

I hadn't come to the doctor's office (that was frankly a massive inconvenience to get to, involving three trains and a bus) to have a strange man question my up-bringing. I didn't have any deep inner turmoil caused by a past disaster that needed to be brought back to the surface. I hadn't been kept in a well or forced to act as a lightning rod for a crazy uncle's science experiments or whatever it is that therapists would like to connect with mania in later life. I didn't have time for these obvious questions. I was broken *now*, it was a recent thing, so let's deal with that, please.

In these first bouts of therapy, each session started with having to fill in the craziness form. The craziness

---

* We are getting to the anxiety bit I promise, hang in there, this is subtext. At least I think it's subtext, it may just be me rambling at the moment. Anyway, subtext.

form quantifies your level of batshit from low (not batshit) to high (too batshit). (Sidenote: it's not called the craziness form, it's a Cognitive Behavioural Therapy assessment form, which analyses your state of mind in an easy numeric scale, but that's not as catchy, is it?) Every time I filled in the form, I was getting top marks, which on one hand I was quite weirdly pleased with as it was the only test that I had aced in my life, but on the other hand it meant I was bonkers.* Eventually I think the strange man got bored of hearing me talk: he informed me that our sessions were over and that I was to take this medication for the foreseeable future. He told me I had 'severe depression' and then said to me . . .

'If I were you, I would be depressed too.'

How comforting! (Sidenote: if you're not happy with your therapist, always ask for another referral – getting the perfect therapist can be like dating; you may have to go through a few duds before you find the one perfect for you.) I left with my prescription form and thought of it as my golden ticket to the chocolate factory: 'This, THIS, will sort out every problem in my life,' I said, as I tried to recreate that bit where Charlie Bucket runs home from the shop. That's a lie, I didn't

---

* Once again I apologise for using derogatory terms for mental illness, but I'm pretty sure you are allowed to say bonkers if you are bonkers.

do that, I lit a cigarette and stood in the rain waiting for a bus. Real life is nothing like the movies. If my life were a movie it would probably be something like this:

[OPEN, EXTERIOR, BUS STOP, DAY]

Our hero stands at an empty bus stop, a cigarette hanging out of his mouth as Elliott Smith plays in the background. It's raining. The bus arrives, he boards, Elliott Smith keeps playing, it's still raining. He gets off the bus and then boards the train to King's Cross. Elliott Smith keeps playing, it's still raining. Now our hero is back to his house. Elliott Smith is still playing, he's drenched. End. This movie is awful. Budget? £600 million. *Rotten Tomatoes* score? You can decide for yourself. Directed by Uwe Boll probably because that's what I deserve.

At this time my version of normality meant getting through a single day without feeling like I had failed at being a human being. Just one day without finding normal human activities utterly bewildering, without finding panic around every corner, without feeling like a disappointment as a member of society or like an utter failure of a person. People – you know, Other People – operated in a way that felt completely alien to me. They went out and had conversations, drinks, experiences, with people! All of these things terrified me. I chain-smoked so my lips were too busy to deal with small talk. To me, small talk was an obstacle course of inevitable disaster. The other person would say, 'How's work?' and my brain would helpfully whisper: 'Pssst! They don't care about your work, they are looking for a way out of this conversation because you are so boring, you are insignificant, they cannot wait to stop talking to you.' Every social encounter felt like a job interview: I would sweat through my shirt, I drank to try to lubricate my anecdotes, I ran outside at any chance for another cigarette as I knew this would mean I was alone, never mind all the toilet breaks I had to take. When your brain is your worst enemy, you spend a lot of time wanting to be alone, being alone and absolutely hating being alone.

I've never strived to be normal. The dictionary definition of normality only exists in BBC One shows your mum watches, where everyone lives in a tiny picturesque village and the biggest problem they have to deal with that week is that Terry has bought the wrong tablecloth for the village fete and hilarious consequences ensue. But, and I don't know why, I did want to be human, and everyone else made being a human look so easy. People would speak with such fluidity, yet my speech was quiet, forced, uninteresting. Outside of social situations I found myself ignoring reality, unable to deal with bills or mail of any description, as I knew that if I couldn't pay them I would be branded a failure. I stopped checking my bank balance, and I relied instead on the tested method of hoping money would appear out of the machine when I asked for it, terrified that one day all that the machine would provide was dust, and a horrifying sense of financial incompetence. I blamed it all on the depression. I had made myself out to be 'the depressed man'. I envisaged myself as the troubled genius, when in fact I was just a troubled nobody. I didn't have any talents, any skills, anything that set me apart from any other person with this condition. It was more the rationale of 'There must be a reason this is happening to me', trying to find excuses instead of accepting that this was part of who I was, and that this was something that couldn't be fixed or mended, but was something I could learn to live with, learn to control and learn to be human with.

As I fell deeper into the persona of the Sad Depressed Man, I ignored everything else in my life. Relationships fell away, opportunities passed me by. Mental health conditions are inherently selfish. You spend so much of your life worrying about yourself that it's hard to direct your focus outwards. This is why I never saw the anxiety coming. I had already committed myself to one disorder, so I thought surely this must be the all-encompassing problem with my mind. It never occurred to me that the human brain is a complicated supercomputer where various issues can be happening at once. I regarded it as one problem that I needed to fix, not several that needed tending to at the same time.

When I started coming to terms with my depression, when I accepted and tried to own it, I noticed that it wasn't the only thing plaguing me. I read countless books on the subject, I spoke to other depressives, and things just simply didn't add up. The problem with only getting one diagnosis is – though I am loath to speak a bad word about anyone in the medical profession as they have saved me more times than I care to mention – sometimes they don't get the whole diagnosis.

Step Two: Anxiety

I was told I had severe depression four years before I was diagnosed with severe anxiety. Mental health conditions are often pretty good like that: buy one get one totally unwanted item free! The psychological equivalent of getting to the counter only to be told this item is on offer and you have to pick up another. The queue is behind you, you just want this to be over, but now you have to rummage through the store as the queue grows longer due to your inability to read a label. You don't even want the second pack of microwaveable rice but you don't want the cashier to think you're rejecting their help.

It took a while to come to terms with the fact that I was a depressive, so you can imagine my glee when the doctor said social anxiety, general anxiety disorder and separation anxiety were also on the table now. This is when I threw myself at Cognitive Behavioural Therapy (CBT). Even though I had had therapy before, CBT is less Freudian questions about your mum, and more focused on changing your behavioural patterns. I had, in my mid-twenties, realised that I couldn't do this by myself. I had just met my now wife, and hiding the crazy was taking a lot out of me. I needed help and I could finally admit that.

I'd heard the term 'feeling anxious' before. I just never knew that anxiety, real full-blown life-altering anxiety, was a thing. I had been anxious before, I had panicked in airports because I felt like I had lost my passport even though I knew exactly which pocket it was in. I had sent text messages and got no response, causing myself to panic about the inevitable consequences I was inventing in my own mind. But I had just simply never associated 'being anxious' with anxiety. I could understand depression through memoirs I had read of tortured artists, but I had never encountered the equivalent for anxiety. Maybe that was my own ignorance, or maybe it's a social stigma ingrained in all of us that we treat anxiety on the same scale that we treat worry. That we are just overreacting, that we are hypersensitive or, from a male perspective as I have been told many times, acting like a girl. (The idea that weakness is an inherently female attribute is a completely sexist idea that needs to be addressed in its own chapter, but we'll leave that for now and basically conclude that the oversimplification of mental health disorders and their equivalence with outdated gender roles is a position taken only by fuckwits.) Basically, I didn't know shit about anxiety, so I didn't know what I was dealing with.

At a very basic level, and we will break this down more later I promise, anxiety is worry on steroids. Worry is actually very useful. It's a perfectly natural human reaction to everyday situations, and helps us determine how we approach events in our lives. It is – to put it simply – an act of self-preservation. Worry is an evolutionary default: we panic because we sense a threat and our senses become heightened in case we need to escape. We sweat because we pre-empt panic with the need to flee, and in the animal kingdom at least, sweating helps your body regulate itself if you find yourself in the unfortunate position of having to flee a predator. These were all incredibly helpful attributes to have when we were evading the unwanted attentions of a sabre-toothed tiger, but when your main problem that day is 'I have to give a presentation at work', having the chemicals in your brain tell you that you need to run for your life and that everything you know is about to come to an end can become more of a hindrance than a help.

I had finally managed to get my depression under some sort of control. I say control; I had wrangled it into submission, we were on even terms now, I understood it. I could finally make fun of it, which gave me power over it. I had moved to London in this time, I had met the love of my life, and she understood my craziness and helped me contain it. But as my depression took a back seat my new friend, anxiety, assumed it was his turn to kick my arse. As I had no previous knowledge of anxiety, I never knew it was a condition that could take your life and punch it right in its face. I started finding it difficult to be around people. I found it difficult to do my job. I found it difficult to go outside.

I had to take time off work. I made excuses to get out of commitments. I was effectively turning myself into a weird little hermit of my own invention.

The perfect ally of mental health problems is complacency: you self-medicate with biscuits and blankets and sixteen seasons of a weird foreign cartoon you found on YouTube and don't quite understand but the lack of story structure gives you a glorious sense of freedom. You regard what is obviously a problem with complete apathy and this only results in the condition getting worse. So I had a stern word with myself. I went out. I went to work. I spoke to people. It was all awful, every moment of it was horrible, all I wanted to do was run, flee in any way I could, but I did it. Every interaction, every decision felt like the moments before a disaster. I had full-on anxiety attacks in airports, train stations, at work. A complete lack of control of a situation resulted in me turning into a furious puddle of my former self. I continued to attempt to operate as a normal human being, as if I was some sort of undercover spy among a completely different species, terrified that one day I would be uncovered as a fraud. In the years that followed, my anxiety stayed with me like an ugly rash I couldn't find a cure for, and my depression appeared now and again just to remind me that he was still paying for the room he'd rented in my brain.

Despite this I asked my girlfriend to marry me, and she said yes. Well, I downplayed that a bit: once I had drunk enough to convey a certain air of humanity, I asked my girlfriend to marry me. The morning of the big day I was petrified. I stood outside the venue and chain-smoked, hoping not to be asked any more questions. I put on my suit and stood in a room while the registrar ran me through how the service would work. My face went bright red, I started sweating. While blushing is often viewed as an endearing feature, for many actually doing it it is a humiliating reaction. The body, without your permission, tells the world that your emotions are having a field day. Be it good or bad, the brain just screams FUCK YOU and makes your face bright red, just because it can. I got through the service in one piece, if not a bit worried that all our wedding pictures would feature my beautiful wife and some sort of bright red sweaty ham man standing next to her with a look of abject fear on his gormless face.

But for what is supposed to be one of the most stressful days of your life, our wedding was a great day for me. I was running on so much adrenaline (and nice whisky) that I can't remember feeling anywhere near the level of anxiety I had felt as I stood waiting before the service. I actually managed to go several hours without once thinking about it. I was accomplishing the things I had seen the normal people on Facebook do, so naturally I fooled myself into thinking that this was it, this was my way onto the path of normality. Some movies tie themselves up nicely, the plot points all have closure, the character arcs are enjoyable and it just ends. Hooray! But then, for some reason, they just have to make a sequel, an unnecessary sequel no one asked for. This is a very convoluted way of saying my anxiety came back.

I had my first ever panic attack after I dropped a mug in the kitchen. Because that's a perfectly reasonable thing to have a panic attack about apparently. Until this my anxiety had been a constant hum in the background; this was the unexpected crescendo. Panic attacks are great because they make no sense and are completely stupid and need to get in the fucking bin.* Being a rational human, I instantly leapt to the informed deduction that I was having a heart attack and was going to die alone on my kitchen floor. The police would come in and find a broken mug and assume I had been bludgeoned to death with a My Little Pony ceramic beverage container.† Then they would think I was a brony (one of those people who want to bang cartoon horses, do not Google that at work, actually just don't Google it at all) as well. All of this was going through my head as I lay slumped on the floor, wheezing like an air bed under a hydraulic press, my heart beating so fast I thought it was going to jump out of my chest like an alien (an alien from the movie *Alien* obviously, not like an alien from the movie *Space Jam*).

---

* Also panic attacks make no evolutionary sense, there is never a situation in which the human body needs to go 'You know what, let's fucking shut everything down and be a twat for a bit'. Evolution is stupid.

† A quick note, the My Little Pony mug is my wife's . . . was my wife's . . . basically it isn't/wasn't mine. Not that there's anything wrong with men liking My Little Pony, what you do in your life is between you and your browser history.

So after about five minutes of thinking I was dying, coming to terms with my own existence, getting extremely angry about what an inconvenience this was, I managed to get my breath under control, my heart slowed back to its usual beat and I sat up, although in a heap, on the kitchen floor. My chest physically hurt from the workout my lungs had just put me through. As this was my first panic attack, I had no idea what it was when it was happening. I, as a complete idiot, didn't want to trouble anyone else with these health problems, so I did the exact thing I am going to tell you not to do: I checked my symptoms online. After sixteen diagnoses telling me I had a brain tumour, five telling me I had brain parasites and one telling me I was giving birth, I found the section of the NHS website on panic attacks. 'A panic attack occurs when your body experiences a rush of intense psychological (mental) and physical symptoms.' Cool, so I couldn't have had a panic attack, because normal people don't have panic attacks about dropping a mug, they have panic attacks because the bomb with the timer counting down is at ten seconds and they don't know whether to cut the red or green wire, or something equating to that level of extreme stress.

My next panic attack happened on a rush hour tube. While still a massive inconvenience, I could understand the rationale behind having a panic attack on the tube – it made more sense to me than having one as a reaction to dropping a mug. I've never liked public transport: it's too loud, too cramped, it's full of people and people are generally awful. A packed rush hour tube on a Thursday night is my third least favourite place in the world. (My second least favourite place in the world is any funeral ever because funerals are . . . funerals, and my first least favourite place is a bar I have gone into for a quiet pint only to discover that 'the game' is on and I now have to endure the confusing enthusiasm of a sport I do not understand.) As this was my second panic attack I figured I knew what to do. 'This isn't my first rodeo,' I thought to myself, and then started thinking that only people who have ever gone to a rodeo are technically allowed to say that and it feels unfair as it's a good saying but I have no inclination to ever attend a rodeo. So once again, I acted rationally and calmly. I launched myself off the hectic tube car, knocking over several innocent commuters and at least three Spanish tourists,* and sat on a bench on the platform trying to wrestle my breath back into my lungs. One thing guaranteed to freak people out on a public transport system is if you run from a tube car while sweating more than a BBC DJ hearing their name in the news for the first time in fifteen years, screaming like a hen trapped in a cement mixer. Five minutes of confusing hysteria and irrational chest pain passed and I was back to normal. Well, as normal as I can be.

The third panic attack happened while I was sat in a busy bar with my wife. Nothing says 'romantic evening

---

* Fun fact: at any one time in London, you will be unknowingly touching at least three Spanish tourists.

out' like your husband having a full on emotional breakdown while the table next to you does flaming sambuca shots. The noise, the crowds, the everything of the bar, was all too much. After that night I started having panic attacks every few weeks. I fell back into the pattern of not wanting to go out because the unbearable fear of going outside, thinking that absolutely anything – no matter how minuscule or bizarre – could trigger another panic attack, was all I could think about. I could feel my mind falling apart again.

But the one thing that has always made me feel somewhat normal in this world is reading what other sufferers have gone through, how they manage to operate – that was, and still is, a form of therapy for me. The knowledge that I am not the only person in the world whose brain is trying to trip them up at every turn is what keeps me sane. And that's how I found the Internet.

I had never thought of the Internet as an outlet for my mental health problems, or imagined that the Internet would help me. The Internet is really just a forum of people screaming 'NO' at each other while someone looks at porn in the corner. But I spent the hours when I couldn't sleep (anxiety doesn't let you sleep, it's like a newborn child, without all the pooping but with more red wine) reading articles on mental health. I started talking about it on Twitter and I never expected the response I received. Just hearing one person say 'I've gone through this' or 'As someone with this problem, I can tell you that it gets better' was a massive relief. I kept talking about my depression, my anxiety, and people replied, people wrote about their issues, stories were shared, I started to feel less like I was alone with this problem.

Communication is vital when it comes to mental health issues. If we can talk about it, we can normalise it and we can feel less like outsiders. Living with anxiety is already tiring enough without the weight of feeling lonely with it. Anxiety means you are constantly arguing with yourself, constantly feeling as if you are not doing enough and failing at tasks most people complete with ease, so knowing that you are not alone in this is crucial. I may not have 'cured' my anxiety, as I don't believe such conditions can miraculously go away, but I believe you can learn to cohabit with them, to turn the volume down on them. I still have panic attacks, I still find going out and being sociable a terrifying experience, but I can do it. This isn't a book to cure you of your ills, this isn't a self-help book or a very long motivational speech packaged between irreverent metaphors, this is a 'how to start looking after yourself' book, this is a 'reminder that you can do this' book.

This is just a basic guide to survival.

2.
A BEGINNER'S GUIDE TO ANXIETY
(AKA Science, Hugh Grant and Moomins)

'Today hasn't been too bad, has it?'

'Well . . .'

'No, come on, it hasn't been that bad.'

'Maybe we should think about this for a few hours, I'm sure we can figure out how you've fucked it up somewhere.'

'Do we have to?'

'Oh my, yes.'

Aristotle referred to early ideas of mental health problems as 'diseases of the soul'. Kierkegaard said anxiety is a natural state of being – he thought that if our lives were completely predetermined we would suffer no form of anxiety. He, in his confusing and Danish way, said: 'Anxiety is a dizziness of freedom.' While battling his own anxiety, Freud said that anxiety is 'not a simple thing to grasp', but then Freud tried to cure his own anxiety by taking fuckloads of cocaine so I'm not entirely sure how helpful he is here . . .

As of the last count, 18% of the US population suffer with some form of anxiety,* with 13% of us Brits suffering too. One in four people will battle a mental health problem at some point during their lives, yet depression, anxiety, obsessive–compulsive disorder, PTSD are all weaknesses in the ever-watching eyes of the popular narrative. It can be difficult to differentiate between our stereotypical views of mental health and the reality of them. It is possible to form an idea of what they are even without experiencing them, but if popular culture doesn't provide a realistic look at these conditions the stereotypes will continue to survive. Depression isn't a romantic feeling of melancholy that can be cured by travelling the world and falling in love with a French bartender called Jean-Luc who has giant pecs and a hairy chest and . . . I've lost my train of thought here. Oh yeah, OCD isn't just flicking on and off a light switch seventeen times before leaving a room, or needing to be tidy. You don't always get PTSD from staring at a ceiling fan that for some reason then starts playing helicopter sound effects. And anxiety isn't the adorable Hugh Grant character falling over his words and being delightfully awkward. The portrayals of mental health disorders are so clichéd because the

* http://www.thekimfoundation.org/html/about_mental_ill/
  anxiety.html

realities are uncomfortable. It's pretty obvious that people would rather watch an anxious Hugh Grant blush and stutter than an anxiety-ridden Hugh Grant who can't leave the house for six weeks and is now terrified of open spaces. But before we end up in a spiral of deconstructing the damaging effects on humanity of 90s romcoms, let's swerve back to the topic at hand.

Anxiety crashes into your brain in many different forms: Generalised Anxiety Disorder, OCD, separation anxiety, phobias, social anxiety . . . the list goes on and on and on. There is a rumour that if you manage to collect all the different types of anxiety you get a letter of congratulation from the Queen. Eight million people in the UK suffer with some form of anxiety at any one time. That's enough people to fill a hundred sports stadiums, although they probably wouldn't go to the stadiums because the stadiums would be too busy and loud and generally awful for anyone with any form of anxiety. To the anxious mind, anything can be a trigger. There is no logic behind it; everyone perceives threats in different guises, so everyone feels anxiety differently. While it is a common disease, it is bizarrely unique. As it is so unique, there's no single remedy to fix those eight million people. After years of experimenting I have found that the easiest coping mechanism for me is 60% being medicated up to my tits and 40% ignorance and stubbornness. It's important here to say that what works for one person rarely works for another sufferer. The road to 'normality' is paved with trial and error, and it can be more error than anything else.

DISCLAIMER: The following paragraph is a crude guide to the science of anxiety, I will go into this in more detail later on (and ask an actual human scientist about it too), but for now, let's just get a rough idea of what the fucking hell is going on up there.

The human threat centre of the brain is the amygdala; it's what keeps us alert and aware of our surroundings. It is an extremely important part of our anatomy, but like most things in life, it can be a dick at times for no bloody reason. In evolutionary terms our amygdala was vital to our survival. It's the reason we evolved from cavemen into the Netflix-obsessed, skinny-jeans-wearing monsters we are today. When our cavemen cousins were foraging for berries or trying to avoid being eaten to death by giant wombats or something, our amygdala saved us. When we thought about shoving our faces into a fire or tickling a mammoth's undercarriage it was the thing that screamed: 'DON'T DO THAT, YOU DICK.' It brought common sense. Without our amygdala we would see a salivating tiger staring at us from across the plains and stand there completely nonplussed. With our amygdala, we knew we had to fucking leg it before Tigger started using our entrails as a plaything.

As the years passed our natural threats changed: the threats of war, disease, premature death, financial collapse . . . In a very short time, we went from panicking about tiger attacks to panicking that our bank card would be refused. This is where our amygdala has been a bit of a dick. Instead of keeping up with the advances in society that have taken most of our perceived threats away, the amygdala simply sees the same level of threat in new places, and as we are built to flee from predators, it thinks that we should have that exact same emotional and physical reaction when stood on a full tube car. When the amygdala senses a threat (Tigger- or tube-related) in whatever way, shape or form, it shouts 'THIS IS MY MOMENT' and floods our bodies with cortisol and adrenaline. These chemicals ooze from our adrenal glands, and the adrenaline tightens our muscles, makes our hearts go faster, makes us sweat and does everything we need to get ready to fucking run. Cortisol works in a similar way, but is responsible for our blood pressure and metabolism in situations of stress or danger. At the same time, our brain stops creating serotonin, a neurotransmitter that controls our moods. High levels give us a good mood; low levels, a bad mood, hence why low levels of serotonin are equated with depression. So as your body puts itself into fight or flight mode (heart racing, cortisol overflowing like champagne at a Tory austerity conference) our serotonin as low as a Tory's morals, (OK enough Tory analogies) . . . we panic, we try our best to figure out what the fuck the threat is, we get drenched in fear, and this is the root of anxiety. It's an evolutionary fuckup, an overcompensation that once defined us as a dominant species, but now makes it difficult for some of us to make eye contact with people.

To let you know that I am not talking shit, and that

I do actually suffer with this complete head nonsense, this is what is going on in my noggin right now.

I just need to take a deep breath. OK. Let's do this.

In the anxiety sweepstakes I have managed to win GAD (General Anxiety Disorder), social anxiety, separation anxiety, insomnia, dermatophagia (ripping the skin off your fingers) and a completely irrational phobia of Moomins. This is not a joke. I fucking hate Moomins. We will skip over the self-mutilation of my fingers for a moment and focus on these bizarre albino hippo bastards. A lot of people who know me in real life think my fear of Moomins is hilarious, and that I can't be 'that weird', which just proves how little they know me. Be under no illusion here, I am severely weird. For instance, I was once walking through Notting Hill with my wife and noticed a full-size Moomin in a shop window. I ran. In terms of fight or flight, I would conclude that this was quite a violent flight reaction. My brain saw something it perceived as a threat, and its most reasonable reaction was to fucking leg it down a busy high street. What makes it worse is that my style of running can only be compared to that of a ketamine-addled giraffe that has somehow found itself on an ice rink.

For anyone unaware of Moomins, they feature in a series of Swedish children's books that were turned into a cartoon invented by Satan to mentally scar human beings and to punish humanity for all of our misdoings. My irrational fear began when I saw an episode entitled 'The Groke' as a child. The Groke was a terrifying being that appeared in the distance as the main characters watched it out of their window. Every time they closed the curtains and then reopened them, the Groke was closer. I never fully recovered. I should sue somebody for this. The only reason I don't go through with this lawsuit is that I assume the company that makes Moomins would pay all damages with Moomin merchandise and just the thought of that makes my brain cry. The fear of a cartoon is kyrofelonoshophobia (try saying that three times quickly while drunk), and this is my unique phobia. Even having searched the Internet for quite some time I've never found anyone else who had a severe phobia of Moomins, so my attempt to start a support group ended before it began. All of our anxieties are individual; we are all that little bit weird, be it being scared of snakes, spiders, responsibility or cartoons from the 80s. This is why there is no singular cure, no tablet that can fix everyone. It's important to differentiate between a fear and a phobia: a fear of snakes or spiders, for example, is inherent. We recognise these as threats to ourselves, so it is completely rational to be wary of them. However, a phobia of spiders, as opposed to a fear, is the difference between being terrified by a black widow on your shoulder (rational: a credible threat to yourself) and being terrified by a money spider on the other side of the room (irrational: money spiders won't hurt you, they are just going about their business, leave them be). Most phobias are simple defence mechanisms. You may have a fear of sharks because sharks are massive and have huge teeth and the movies say they eat people (important reminder: sharks don't eat people all that often, they are more scared of us than we are of them, this may mean that sharks have anxiety), or a fear of heights as heights – or, more specifically, falling from them – kill people. But when the phobias become irrational, that is our overactive amygdala being a complete shit. There is no real threat about a Moomin, it is almost impossible for a Moomin to cause me physical harm, unless a massive statue of one falls on me or something, which is now going to keep me awake for WEEKS. Yet this is how my brain sees it, it translates something I once saw as scary or traumatic and makes sure that I am prepared next time I see it. You get scared of the Moomin once, next time your brain will make sure you are ready to get the fuck out of there by making your body go crazy. It makes sense. It's fucking stupid, but it makes sense.

Let's move on to social anxiety, one of the most common conditions. To put it plainly, it's the fear of any social situation. Complicated stuff I know but try to keep up with me here. You are more than likely to recognise some of the weirdness in the next, less-Moomin-related part, so let's see what fun types of anxiety you might have!

First, humans are already awful. We are. All of us. Have you ever been outside? It's a dreadful place filled with walking meat beings herding each other around while they try to mate with one another and produce even more walking meat beings, and the circle continues until chucking-out time at the pub and starts again the next morning.

I don't equate social anxiety with being antisocial. Being an antisocial person means you simply don't want to interact with anyone out of choice, not out of fear or dread. Being antisocial is based in arrogance, while social anxiety is based in terror. The problem here is that if you suffer with social anxiety you can come across as antisocial. You make excuses for not going out,* you find it difficult to talk to people, the idea of a conversation focusing on you makes you sweat, being out of your comfort zone makes you panic. It's far from arrogant to feel this way but for those who don't understand, it can be misconstrued as such.

How long has social anxiety existed? Well, compared to general anxiety disorder, social anxiety seems to be a relatively new disorder. It first made the *Diagnostic and Statistical Manual of Mental Disorders* (or *DSM*, often referred to as the definitive bible for mental health conditions) in 1968, under the guise of 'social fears', and then again in 1980, in the DSM third edition, as a 'social phobia'. It may be that social anxiety has only been recognised so recently (in the last few hundred years) because the threat centre of our brain is unable to deal with the lack of larger or more 'real' threats in our day-to-day lives in modern life; our brain then panics

---

* My favourite excuse I ever used to avoid socialising was in a text that simply read 'I stood on my dog's foot today and he was really upset by it so I should probably stay home and look after him.'

and creates new threats to fill the gaps where the old threats are supposed to be.

My adventures in social anxiety have only been prevalent for the last three years. Before that I was outgoing. I was constantly in the pub, I loved meeting new people, I basked in the joy of being the group clown, knowing I could make people laugh. Now I can barely sit in a pub with people for fifteen minutes before checking every escape route, barely saying anything, avoiding telling any jokes in case no one laughs or any attention comes my way, and if I do say anything it's only to direct the conversation away from me. I acknowledge that this can be perceived as rude, but as I sit in a loud bar, people screaming over the top of each other while I clutch my pint tight into my chest, I feel as if my insides are on fire. That at any moment my heart is going to burst from going too fast.

One of my therapists said that this panic derived from my low self-confidence, that if I were to speak to anyone I would instantly assume they found me boring, unfunny, generally a chore to be around. This is true. I automatically make the judgement that whoever I am in contact with feels nothing but disdain for me. In this panic I found the only way to cope: by saying as little as I can. If I don't say anything I can't be judged. I can't be found to be the boring, tragically unfunny human disaster I think I am. It's all down to fear. The fear of being judged unworthy of another human's company, the fear of embarrassment, the fear of being a disappointment. Social anxiety could be a disastrous nonsense caused by an under-evolved amygdala, or it might be a defence mechanism, a chemical-based safety blanket for our minds. With fewer threats in the real world, our brain is attempting to overcompensate, to protect us from newly invented threats, replacing threats to our physical selves with threats to our personalities, our reputations, our sense of self.

Next for me comes GAD (Generalised Anxiety Disorder), the nice blanket name for a myriad of conditions. Anxiety is universal as well as unique, because pretty much everyone will feel anxious at some point in their life. It usually goes hand in hand with stressful events: going to the doctor, job interviews, meeting the in-laws for the first time; the sort of interactions or events we would usually avoid but somehow find ourselves forced into. Feeling anxious is the brain's way of dealing with high-pressure situations. It's normal. The difference between mild anxiety and severe anxiety is the way the brain overanalyses the outcomes of a situation. While a mildly anxious person would think, 'I hope I make a good impression meeting the in-laws for the first time, but I'm a bit nervous,' the severely anxious mind would think, 'Oh God, OK, don't be sick when you meet them, don't accidentally punch the mum in the face, why would we think that? It doesn't matter, oh God are you saying all this out loud? Why are you sweating so much? Did you just accidentally kick the dog? Why are you talking about Chinese politics in the 70s? You're rambling, put your trousers back on.'

GAD is one of the most frequently diagnosed anxiety

conditions in modern society. It is an overarching term for what happens when our brains are trying to deal with a huge number of negative stimuli at any one time. Perfectly normal scenarios quickly become terrifying feats of immense pressure. Commuting becomes a chore, speaking to other humans becomes a nightmare, you quickly begin to hate yourself and fall victim to your own absurdity. Then five years have passed and you're a hermit person living in a pillow fort in your messy apartment who only communicates with other human beings through Twitter or a series of semaphore-like arm movements to a human in the apartment opposite. Too over the top? GOOD. Now you're starting to understand my brain; we're on the same page. Once again, on a chemical level GAD is down to too much cortisol and adrenaline, and a lack of serotonin. It's the art of seeing danger everywhere, and your brain blue-screening like a defective laptop you bought from a car boot sale.

The next winner on our list is separation anxiety. The anxious mind will only find peace in a comfort zone. Something familiar. Something safe. Nine times out of ten this will be the anxious person's bed. It's an area we control, so it's an area where we feel comfortable and secure. I have spent a large percentage of my anxious hours safely nested in my bed, surrounded by biscuits and binge-watching bad American shows about beautiful people who find themselves in situations beautiful people wouldn't usually find themselves in. For the anxious, constants are important. A stable space that doesn't change, a space we can count on to be the same every time we return to it. Separation anxiety is the feeling of being ripped away from this safety blanket. It can be a place or a person, but the anxiety comes from a certainty suddenly becoming an uncertainty.

Separation anxiety is most common between babies and mothers. The kid has grown up with the mother as a constant, so prolonged periods of separation cause distress. This is of course an important part of becoming a fully-fledged human person, as we learn independence and taxes and stuff. However, it is thought that this early separation can also be the root of separation anxiety within adults; as with phobias, the brain remembers a traumatic event and works its hardest to prevent that from happening again. We've all met couples where one can never do anything without the other, but we'll let Freud cover that. Adults usually grow out of this (unless you're a bit Norman Bates, in which case this book may not be strong enough to help you understand that problem, I'd recommend a good therapist or barman) and learn to cope with a certain level of uncertainty in their lives. However, if your brain can only function properly in one scenario, when that scenario is uncertain in some way, the brain panics, it malfunctions, it breaks, because the human brain is a moron.

My separation anxiety stems from a process of routine. I am calm in my routine. I plan things, I plan them meticulously and to a bizarre level of detail. My levels of uncertainty come from a change to this routine. I know this sounds more like obsessive–compulsive disorder (another, if not more extreme, form of anxiety) but I refuse to be one of those people who trivialises a serious mental health condition by saying, 'Yeah, I'm a little bit OCD.' No, you're not OCD. You're fussy. You like things neat. You're not OCD. Keeping your living room tidy is slightly different to a life-altering series of physical and emotional tics with nonsensical triggers and no off switch.

Anyway: a break in my routine, or a wrinkle in a plan I have created, can result in anxiety and sometimes panic attacks for me. For instance, I leave the house at the same time every morning, I walk to the tube stop, I know exactly where to stand on the platform so when I have to change tubes at London Bridge my door is exactly next to the connecting walkway between platforms. I know the London Underground in a bizarrely accurate way, so can happily make detours if need be, but one morning I removed my headphones to hear the train announcer saying, 'This train will not stop at London Bridge due to overcrowding.' Fine, I thought to myself, I can change at Waterloo and it will only be a five-minute difference. I could feel my heart going faster but I controlled my breathing and put my headphones back on. At Waterloo the train announcer came on again: 'Waterloo station has no access to the Northern Line due to a signal failure, please find another route.' This is when my mind lost it and that comedy sound effect of a record scratch went off in my brain. My original plan had failed. My backup plan had failed. I exited the train and sat on the bench on the platform, wheezing as I felt my blood pressure rise, quickly tapping my fingers against my palms in an attempt to give me something to focus on. This is separation anxiety: it is irrational panic that makes you look like a hyperventilating penguin on a train platform during rush hour.

Now for insomnia. Insomnia is a common side effect of anxiety, not a full-blown type of anxiety. However, if you've had anxiety for some time, you will know that sleep is for the weak. This is what I would tell myself as I sat at 3 a.m. staring into my computer researching the history of the Great Australian Emu War.* Trapped in another Wikipedia hole because my brain refused to shut down. My days consist mostly of feeling tired all day, sluggishly making it through work in a haze of seemingly self-imposed exhaustion. I get home and promise myself that this will be the night that I get an early night. Inevitably, I lie in bed staring at the ceiling either pondering the most absurd things: 'Do dogs think in woofs?', 'If I could fly where would I go?', 'If a toy in *Toy Story* dies, the human wouldn't notice because they are always still when they come in the room anyway, so would the other toys know? Would the human be playing with the corpse of one of their friends and they couldn't do anything about it?' I either continue to ponder these abstract concepts or my brain goes into nostalgia mode and starts remembering every

* Yes you read that right, it was a war where the Australian army waged war on the emu population and lost.

embarrassing thing I have ever done. This is brilliant because not only do you have to relive embarrassment first-hand and third-hand at the same time, but you get to lie there for hours thinking up every possible scenario that could have happened if only one tiny element of the story had changed.

For some reason my anxious brain comes alive at night. I have spent months living on two hours' sleep a night. I started developing a twitch in one eye due to lack of sleep, which just makes you look like a maniac when you're trying to hold an important work meeting and you keep inadvertently winking at people. Insomnia isn't as cool as the movie *Fight Club* made it out to be. You don't get an imaginary friend who starts a successful soap business with you (*Fight Club* spoiler alert, but if you haven't seen it, it came out about like fifty years ago what is wrong with you). Insomnia leaves you as a shell of a human. Or just more of a shell of a human than you were before. The only bonus of insomnia that I can think of is that if you are going for the 'gaunt Christopher Lee circa 1980 look' you've got it nailed. I tried everything: meditation, not looking at any screens (TV, phone, laptop) for hours before bed to avoid stimuli, valerian root, those sprays you put on your pillow that make your pillow smell like your gran's house and that is in some way supposed to be relaxing – until eventually a very nice doctor gave me sleeping pills. The one drawback with this was that as a human who wasn't used to long bouts of sleep, I then felt perpetually befuddled. The pills worked for a few months before my body got used to them, but for those few months I would sleep like a baby. Which is a terrible expression if you think about it, I don't know much about kids, but I know that they don't sleep at all. In fact every new parent I know looks like I did when I had insomnia. But clichéd sayings aside, I obtained some sleep by drugging and drinking myself to unconsciousness, somewhat unsuccessfully*.

The last major ingredient in my anxiety cocktail is dermatophagia, or, in its simplest form, biting your fingernails. I have bitten my nails since I was a kid; my mother tried the weird nail polish that made your fingernails taste like a chemical explosion in an arse factory but it didn't stop me. As I got older and my anxiety became all-encompassing, I started chewing the skin around my nails – my nails were by now barely visible due to a high amount of rodent-like gnawing, and this was the next step. Whenever I felt uneasy or uncomfortable, I would rip the skin off my fingers with my teeth. My fingers were permanently bleeding and I would get through several layers of skin until the colour went from red just underneath the skin, to the purple layer under that, to the light pink layer under that. And every time they bled, I bit more. Every part of it was painful, but my brain ignored it, it was a masochistic coping mechanism. I spent years with my fingers covered in bloody plasters and band-ages, I made excuses for why my hands were like this

* THIS IS NOT A BRILLIANT LONG-TERM PLAN.

– 'An accident at work' or 'I trapped my hand in the car door again' – but really I was cannibalistically punishing myself. I don't do this when my mind is calm, and my mother now knows how I am feeling by simply analysing my fingers. If they are smooth and barely scarred she knows I am coping, if they are bleeding and covered in blood blisters she asks me how I am. Most of my digits are permanently scarred from this. My thumb on my right hand no longer has a crease at the joint, the skin has been removed so many times it's now a smooth ugly sausage that lives just off my palm. Anxiety manifests itself physically in bizarre ways, always masochistic. The incessant pulling of your own hair (trichotillomania), a complete lack of sleep, twitches and tremors, or even self-harm. This is effectively what I had been doing. Self-harming, just not in the traditional sense.

For someone with such a myriad of anxiety problems I have managed to miss some of the more obvious phobias. I have no problem with flying, but the stress of an airport makes me break down. Small spaces make me feel safe (if I had the energy and motivation to, I would probably spend a large amount of my time in a pillow fort), large open areas are brilliant until you throw crowds into the mix. Spiders? Fine. Snakes? Weird but don't bother me. They are basically just necks with a face. Moomins? We've been through this. The bizarre irrationality of anxiety is what makes it so hard to understand and even harder to diagnose. Most of the time when you are feeling anxious the response from a friend or family member will be 'Stop overreacting' or 'You're causing a scene'. To which the correct response is: 'I am not causing a scene, it's you who doesn't seem to grasp the severity of the situation. There are too many people here. It's too loud. That man smells weird. Why would you bring me to a Moomin museum? If I explode from stress and die I am going to come back and haunt you.'

And just for good measure, although it's not technically a form of anxiety, more of a third cousin-twice-removed that turns up to weddings they aren't invited to, is my struggle with imposter syndrome. For those unfamiliar with imposter syndrome, it is the general fear of everyone finding out you have no idea what you're doing because you've faked your way into your place in the world. I have this in spades (wait, who measures things in spades any more?), but the annoying thing is that it is usually only diagnosed among 'high achievers', which is a category I do not think I fit into, even if my friends and wife try to convince me otherwise. I think I am a nobody. High achievers have a Lamborghini and a coke addiction; I have one pair of shoes that are held together with tape and maybe a slightly obsessive like of roast potatoes. If I tried the 'don't you know who I am?' line on someone they would reply with 'No' and 'Please stop chasing the penguins' and 'How did you get into this enclosure?'

Imposter syndrome is a never-ending terror that one day your boss, or your friends, or your partner will realise who you really are. That at some point in the future they will rip off your bad Scooby Doo villain disguise you've made for yourself to hide the anxiety-ridden weirdo you truly are, and it'll turn out you were Mr Davies the creepy old janitor the entire time. Or something. I don't think that metaphor made much sense. Anxiety disorders are particularly good at making you feel worthless, like you don't deserve any of the good things you have received in your life. As a result, imposter syndrome is commonplace. However, as I have said before – though in no way am I trying to trivialise this syndrome – I am entirely convinced that normal people, people who look like they have everything together, are faking it. We are all just trying our best, and our best is just hoping that everyone else doesn't figure out that we're all panicking on the inside.

The one thing to remember is that anxiety doesn't play by your rules, which is why it can be so hard to diagnose. One of the hardest things you can do is to stand face to face with your mental health problem and scream 'FUCK YOU' in its face, or at least, 'You and I will have a long conversation about this when we get home', accompanied by that glare your mum used to do when you were in trouble but also in public. My anxious brain is proficient in ignoring my persistent screams to give me a break, even if it's just for a day or so, but it is important to keep screaming, to keep letting it know that we won't stop screaming at it. Anxiety is erratic, unpredictable and fucking annoying, but the worst thing you can do is pretend that this isn't happening.

So welcome to the anxious brain, it's bloody awful in here.

3.
MY ANXIOUS BRAIN VS. THE MORNING
(AKA Coffee, Mecs and Duvet Nests)

There is only one good bit of the day. It's that glorious moment when your eyes open and reality doesn't exist, all that exists is that you're comfy, you're befuddled, you've got one cold foot because you left it outside of the blanket to regulate your body temperature: it is an ignorant paradise. This moment lasts exactly four seconds before your brain catches up with you and then it's all downhill from there.

'Morning!'
'Can we not?'
'Good night's sleep?'
'You know it wasn't.'
'Why, what happened?'
'What happened? You happened! We went to bed at midnight, lay in the dark having an existential crisis until

3 a.m., got up to get a glass of water, then lay there wondering how our life would be different if we hadn't failed all our exams, or had travelled more, or been good with money.'

'Yeah, but we got some sleep at 5 a.m. for a few hours.'

'It's 6.45 now.'

'Exactly.'

The anxious brain is the enemy of sleep. Anxiety's main function is to create fear and tension in every situation in your life, so it makes sense that the time when you deserve rest is also afflicted with unnecessary pressure. As I mentioned in the previous chapter, a lack of 'real' threats allows the anxious mind to wreak havoc, jumping to wild conclusions such as hearing a creak in your house and automatically assuming a murderer has gained access to your property and is now skulking around in the dark. The anxious brain will evaluate the day, attempting to find anything that went wrong, or that could have been avoided with a little extra thought. Anxiety doesn't see bedtime as a time to power off and cool down before another hectic day; it is a time to scrutinise, to carefully pick your life apart.

As a result of not being able to shut down for seven hours a day, when morning comes, you have to self-medicate with caffeine. It's the only way to even slightly resemble the shell of a human being you now have to pretend to be. But then you're off your mind box on caffeine, which results in a hyperactive brain, which means you can't sleep, and this circle of coffee-infused sleep deprivation goes on until your body falls apart and stops working, like a sex robot that's been left out in the rain. I imagine.

THE RULES OF COFFEE ARE:

1 coffee – Fine

2 coffees – You haven't had much sleep, that's under-standable

3 coffees – OK stop now

4 coffees – Well, of course you're shaking, what did you think would happen?

5 coffees – This is ridiculous

6 coffees – Your boss sends you home because they found you trying to feed biscuits to the printer and crying because the printer is a 'good boy'

The logical solution, and the medically recommended solution, is to cut out the caffeine. A sensible idea, with only two problems: first, no, and second, no. If I had to cut out coffee I would have to move on to cocaine, and I've never fancied myself as a cokehead. Mainly because it's really expensive and also because cocaine is used mainly by people who wear suits to work and who think Coldplay are a rock band and that Borat quotes are still the height of comedy – basically a group of people I don't want to be affiliated with. Exhibit 1, Sigmund Freud used coke to get over his anxiety and he just ended up blaming everything on his mum.

The added issue for me with cutting out coffee is the change to my routine, which is an integral part of my sanity. Changes in routine are a trigger for me, throwing everything into uncertainty. This is why I don't believe in New Year's resolutions; that and because I fundamentally fear change in all its forms. In the early 90s, Walkers changed the ingredients of Quavers (so they tasted 'slightly cheesier') and my reaction was comparable to that of a child who had just found out his parents had been swallowed alive by a panda while on a business trip to Southend. I have refused to eat Quavers ever since this horrendous flavour betrayal. This is why I only own one pair of shoes at a time and wear them until they fall apart. This is why I would eat the same meal for dinner every night if I could. Change is bad. Remember when they changed the mum on *The Fresh Prince of Bel Air*? Exactly.

The reasons for interrupted sleep are numerous and nonsensical: past trauma, sleep disorders (obviously), side effects from new medication (a general rule, which we will come back to in a later chapter, is that if you start on new meds always give yourself two weeks of self-care as those two weeks are usually a wild ride of bizarre symptoms), addictions to coffee, nicotine or alcohol. It can even be down to being sat on your phone before attempting to sleep. It turns out that flooding your brain with information two minutes before trying to rest is a bad idea, but we all do it. My reasons for poor sleep derive from past events that my brain feels the insatiable need to investigate in depth, even though there is no way of reaching any sort of closure for these problems. It's the mental equivalent of a bad cop drama, where the renegade rookie ignores protocol and opens up the cold case to find the killer that no other cop could ever catch. But with less excitement and more embarrassing yourself in front of your peers, and the rookie always solves the case in the end, even if the angry captain never believed in them. The three most common reasons my anxious brain disregards my need for sleep are:

1. The bully
2. The rugby incident
3. The fact that I am crazy

The bully one is an obvious one. A fantastic human trait is the ability to come up with snappy retorts five years after they would have been helpful. In my case, I was fifteen and a boy at my secondary school, in his infinite wit, announced to the entire PE class that I had – and let me remember this correctly – bigger tits than his mum. A fairly obvious attempt at undermining my self-esteem. I was a big kid and my man mecs (most people call them moobs but I prefer a portmanteau of man-breasts and pecs) were large. At the time I just stood on the school basketball court feeling utterly defeated, but in the years since, at 3 a.m., when I have been re-evaluating this conversation, I have invented some fun responses: 'At least mine are real' would have worked, but that makes it seem like I was proud of my massive mecs. But my personal favourite is, 'Well, none of your mates have seen mine', which would have been brutally crushing. You know you're not doing well at life when you can't sleep so you try to articulate devastating insults to a fifteen-year-old moron.

The thing is, this is nowhere near the worst bullying I received in my youth, or the incident that should stick out predominantly in my mind, yet this is the one I fixate on. It's not the physical batterings but the emotional ones that stick with you into your adult life. This is also an excellent segue into the whole sticks and stones nonsense: instead of teaching our children 'Sticks and stones may break my bones but words will never hurt me', it should be changed to the more realistic 'Sticks and stones may break my bones but words are quite psychologically damaging and can really affect my adult life, career and relationships.' Anyway, I'm glad that's out of my system. As anxious people we live with a closer relationship to our emotions, and when our self-confidence or self-esteem are trampled, we take it to heart; this is just another thing our brain will store and bring back for later examination.

Embarrassing night-time thought evaluation number two: The rugby incident. Now this event really sticks with me, as it's more of a public humiliation story. We've all been publicly embarrassed at some point. It's a part of life; you can't come to terms with your own humanity in its entirety until you've felt like you wanted to climb inside yourself and die in front of a large crowd of people. This can be as simple as telling a joke to a group and no one laughing, or peeing yourself at the class assembly in year 3 (. . . anyone? Just me? Fuck you guys). Different things stick with different people. Mine is the first time I ever got to play for the A team in rugby. Unfortunately, being in the A Team didn't mean you got to drive around in a black van and defeat bad guys, it was just the best team out of the players who were available to the school in that year. There were A, B and C, and I fluctuated between B and C because I was a big lad and therefore worked well as a sort of human bollard; but I also had no hand–eye coordination and the attention span of a magpie in a jewellery shop. The first time I got to play on the A Team was when a lot of the other boys were ill, so I was filler, not killer. As any kid with low self-esteem would, I instantly thought: 'This is it, this is how I prove that I am someone.' Needless to say, that never happened. Ten minutes into the second half, I got the ball. I didn't know what to do with it, so I ran. I ran and none of the scrawny kids could take me down. I was like the stone at the beginning of *Raiders of the Lost Ark*: unstoppable and spherical. I saw the try line. I ran and jumped. I put the ball down over the line. In my mind I celebrated that I had just scored a try for the A Team of my school. I then noticed that I hadn't reached the try line. I had reached the ten-metre line. At which point a large group of boys jumped on me and proceeded to trample me, which was probably due.

This is my first memory of a catastrophic failure. I tried my best and my reward was losing the game and also getting piled on by a bunch of angry sweaty boys. The brain takes public humiliation very seriously, it treats it like any other traumatic event and will prepare us and make sure that this never ever happens again. This can be through never engaging in the activity ever again, or it can be the complete other end of the spectrum: dedicating your life to proving the masses wrong, like a great Hollywood comeback movie. The latter is the rarer of these two options – as with any anxious dilemma, the fight or flight mechanism kicks in, and when it comes to damage to self-esteem, social stature or ego, flight is usually the preferred route.

The fight or flight response is what makes us human. Do we deal with the situation at hand or do we get ourselves out of this as quickly as we can and make sure we never do it ever, ever again? And if we flee, we then have to go over the event in our minds to find the triggers that first created this response. What could we have done differently? Was it our fault or just a natural set of circumstances against which we stood no chance? Hindsight is a wonderful thing; we can go over our past humiliations while lying in bed and convince ourselves that if it ever happened again we would know exactly what to do. We can replay all the arguments we've ever had while in the shower and come up with the best responses ever, but this is actually just our brain looking after us, giving us a bit of false comfort. If the situation were to arise again, many of us would, in most cases, react the exact same way, our brains recalling the horror of our previous escapades, and in turn theorising that our reaction last time was the correct one because we 'escaped' the situation, and the cycle starts again. In CBT, immersion therapy is the practice of choosing to deal with these problems. Throwing yourself into those positions once again, and again and again, until your brain starts to deal with them rationally. But we'll get into that later; at this point in the morning I still haven't even got out of bed . . .

SOME TIPS ON GETTING A BETTER NIGHT'S SLEEP:

⚡ **Avoid caffeine after midday.** If you need to have coffee try – oh God I can't believe I am going to say this – decaf. I feel so dirty.

⚡ **Avoid energy drinks after 4 p.m.** Avoid energy drinks in general really. First, very few liquids that you force inside yourself should be luminous orange or bright green. Second, they taste like someone blended a troll doll with laundry detergent and one of those emoji cushions.

⚡ **Give your brain a rest.** Try not to lie in bed with your phone pressed into your eyeballs. Shockingly, having a brightly lit rectangle that has access to most of the knowledge of human existence next to your face in the dark is detrimental to getting to sleep.

⚡ **Try a routine.** We can all be fuckers for staying up until 2 a.m. for no reason, but try to get into bed at the same time every night: read, write, do something that doesn't involve technology beforehand. Look after your noggin.

Exchanging the warmth and comfort of my own duvet nest for another bout of reality is a struggle that takes quite some time to come to terms with each morning. I envy morning people. Actually, I envy people who can do anything without experiencing an inner quandary that dominates your life, but we'll stick with the morning thing for the moment. I have a theory: all morning people are cyborgs planted into our society by an overarching ruling class to make the proletariat feel bad for not enjoying their mornings. As I stand in the kitchenette of the office, hair dishevelled, clothes crumpled as ironing them would mean getting up earlier, throwing the seventeenth sugar into my coffee, chirpy Susan from HR bounces over and starts talking. TALKING. This is a sick practice to inflict upon other humans at any time before 9 a.m. As a matter of fact, the working day timetable in general is a sickening prospect invented by bastards. Mornings shouldn't start until 12 p.m. And working days should last two hours. And weekends should last six days.

Every morning my brain and I have the same conversation:

'Are we getting out of bed today or are you going to mope here like some sort of blanket slug?'
'I'm getting up, just give me a minute.'
'I mean, I don't care either way. At least here we are safe from all the people who hate you and a world that is probably going to be the orchestrator of your demise.'
'Very deep . . .'
'Come on, you've got three tasks to finish today, which you haven't started yet because you put everything off until the last minute, because you're a dick.'
'I don't put things off to the last minute, I just wait for the opportune time to complete the tasks and it so happens they coincide with the moments leading up to a deadline . . .'
'Whatever helps you sleep at night.'
'Oh, very witty.'

What makes starting the day so bad for the anxious brain? It could be a dash of chronophobia (fear of the future and what it may hold) mixed with a little bit of fear of losing control within your own life. I asked journalist, author, snappy dresser and fellow anxiety sufferer Daisy Buchanan what her definition of anxiety was, and she summed it up as:

'Anxiety is being trapped in the present by the fear of the future.'

Which frankly is a more coherent analysis of anxiety than I have managed to achieve in this book so far. The future is unpredictable, unless you believe that time is linear and everything is predetermined and that woman from the fairground who charges £3 for fifteen minutes is accurately in tune with the cosmos, in which case this next bit isn't for you.

Kierkegaard attributed anxiety to the unpredictability of the future: if we all knew what was going to happen in every moment of our lives then we would have nothing to be anxious about. It's the fear of the unknown, the fear of unpredictability, that makes us anxious. He actually thought that anxiety was a good thing as it demonstrated that we were free to make our own decisions. Or were free to be crippled by fear. Yay, freedom! When the anxious mind is tuned in such a way that routine and predictability are safety blankets, it's easy to see how a fear of the future can indeed trap us in the present. (By the way, I still haven't even got out of bed yet.)

The idea of staying in bed all day, ignoring your phone and ignoring the world, has a low risk factor. Risks are exponentially higher from the moment you leave the house. For example, there are many bees outside the house. Far too many bees. I can be assured that the number of bees inside my house is far lower than the number of bees outside my house. The only sensible solution to avoid bees is to never leave my house. On the other hand you have to look at the positives. My landlord won't let us get a dog, because he is a dog-hating villain and should be in prison for hating dogs. But as with the bee scenario, which is a negative, if I don't leave the house, I never get to see dogs. As someone whose main hobby in life is waving at strangers' dogs, this would limit the number of things I enjoy doing outside my home to zero. The downside to waving at strangers' dogs is that they are usually attached to a human, and the human will sometimes wave back, which is a completely unnecessary interaction in my opinion. Your dog and I are sharing a moment, please give us some privacy.

Anxiety feeds on control, and so things that happen outside of your small bubble of control are triggers. Agoraphobia seems like a promising concept for the anxious brain. Yet for some reason it is seen as terribly unhealthy to never leave your house and start drinking your own urine. People are such prudes. It's also very difficult to make a living if you do not leave the house. It's not impossible, you can become a freelance writer, but that pays very little unless you can feed yourself with 'exposure' and 'great opportunities'. Or you can set up an Etsy shop where you make tiny jackets for dogs out of your old clothes, but this takes time and energy and no one wants dog ball gowns made out of XXL blink-182 T-shirts. As anxiety lives on fear, and everything outside is terrifying, it can be easy to fall into a routine where staying inside your home – the place you associate with the least amount of stress and triggers – is a preferable way of life.

Beating this fear is just one step to overcoming your anxiety. I know we shouldn't give out medals for tiny things, but I am completely in favour of little stickers saying 'Got out of bed today' or 'Left the house and went to work when it felt like my brain was on fire'. Tiny victories like these are crucial to beating the anxious mind into submission.

SOME QUICK TIPS ON HOW TO KEEP AGORA-PHOBIC ANXIETY AT BAY:

⚡ **Shower.** Yes, it's a simple thing, but even if you aren't planning to leave the house today, you will have done something.

⚡ **Get dressed.** This will make you feel like you are ready to leave the house, even if you have absolutely no intention of doing so. Similarly to the above, it's about convincing yourself that you are achieving something with your day even if you have already resigned yourself to a day of YouTube videos and a bucketful of toast.

⚡ **Invite a friend round.** You don't have to tidy your house, just a bit of human interaction can give your brain a little bit of calm.

⚡ **Skype.** Don't want to see someone in real life today? Skype someone. FaceTime someone. Call someone. Having someone else to listen to instead of your own thoughts can be invaluable.

⚡ **Plot your routes outside.** This sounds stupid, but it has worked for me so I am putting it in. If you are concerned about going outside or are simply avoiding it entirely, use Google Maps' street view, and do a practice run of whatever walk or journey you need/ want to do. It's a simple activity to pre-empt any triggers that may be out there.

We drag our arses out of bed, we shower, we groom ourselves to a relatively acceptable level to engage in human interaction. We basically put on a disguise to fool other human beings and to avoid unwanted questions. If you leave the house un-showered, looking like you've been dragged through a hedge backwards and upside down, people tend to ask 'Are you OK? You look a little tired' and while this is true, it's not socially acceptable to answer with 'Well actually, JANET, I feel like I haven't slept in six years, my mind is trying to kill me, I find it difficult to enjoy things, I am a human disaster, my neck hurts, I have terrible posture, I haven't checked my bank account in three months but my card keeps working so I am assuming everything is OK. How are you?' When you answer with honesty people have a tendency to either change the conversation, or walk backwards away from you very slowly and then, when they approach a safe distance, run off towards the horizon screaming.

In a perfect world you would be allowed to turn up to work in your pyjamas, bringing your duvet with you, and to watch Netflix while occasionally emerging from your blanket cocoon to steal biscuits. This has two drawbacks.

First, an office full of people in blanket cocoons is a fire hazard and second, the tube is already packed enough without the added inconvenience of hundreds of duvet people. Things that would be greatly improved by being able to wear a duvet in social situations: weddings, all sports ever, going to the cinema, going to the pub, job interviews, partaking in sandwiches, literally everything.

'You're considering taking the duvet to work again aren't you?'
'You don't know me.'
'They already think you're weird, let's not make it worse.'
'Who? Who thinks I'm weird?'
'Everyone?'
'Oh . . .'
'Just try to be less weird than usual today.'
'Don't tell me how to live my life.'

HOW TO ACTUALLY LEAVE THE HOUSE*:

Visualisation
Your brain will easily convince you that staying at home and ignoring reality is the safest option, so before you

---

* These tips may seem patronising, as most of them are telling you things you already know. The problem with the anxious mind is that we actively ignore what is good for us, so these tips aren't so much advice your grandmother would give you, but me shouting at you, and myself, because I need these as much as you do.

leave the house, make a cup of tea, sit down for a moment and go through your day in your head. Plan your travel, plan your day, visualise the positives, analyse the false negatives and prepare yourself for the horrifyingly necessary part of life in between getting out of bed and getting back into bed.

Set goals

Every book about mental health will tell you to set goals throughout your day, and as annoying as this can sound, it actually bloody works. They can be the tiniest goals imaginable – make sure you drink water, make a round of tea for the office, don't get hit by a tram – if you can meet a few of these a day, you will have achieved something. Plus, these goals can only be met if you leave the house.

Rewards

When you are training a dog, you give it incentives with treats and cuddles and by telling it, regardless of gender, that it is a good boy. Thought this section couldn't get any more patronising?! Well here we go! This will work differently for everyone, but I'll use myself as an example. If the daunting prospect of the outside world is imprisoning me in a cloud of self-doubt and duvet cages, I get up, leave for work early and get a good cup of coffee. That's it. That's the incentive I need to start a day – but this will be entirely different for all of us. It could be treating yourself to a walk on a break, a decent lunch, a pint after work; it's whatever you associate with a bit of self-care and reward. You are training your brain to associate new scary things with a sense of accomplishment and pride in yourself. It's difficult, but you can get there.

The most we can do is try our best. I'm not one for the motivational quotes that are thrown at you on Facebook. I don't particularly want to climb a mountain, I can't see myself 'living each day to the fullest' because it seems tiring and very expensive. My definition of a Good Day is getting through it in one piece and not embarrassing myself in a way that will lead to another 3 a.m. brain investigation. The only person who is expecting more from you than you can handle is you. One simple piece of advice that works for anxiety is this: give yourself a fucking break.

4.

MY ANXIOUS BRAIN VS. COMMUTING

(AKA Man-spreaders, Ubers and Bus Milk)

Congratulations! You have left the house and entered the horrible world of human beings. Now it's time for the next horrendous task of the day. Commuting combines so many aspects that can trigger the anxious mind that it's no surprise that sufferers find it a tremendous chore. Small spaces, crowds, the lack of control, the noise: they're all just feeding into the already sensitive sponge that is the anxious brain.

'There are too many people on this platform.'
'I know.'
'I didn't know there were this many people in the world!'
'Please stop talking.'
'If we can't get on this train we will be late.'
'I know.'

'And if we are late, that's the whole day down the drain.'

'I know . . .'

'Why are you breathing so quickly?'

'Because I don't like crowds, you know this.'

'Is it because any of these people could be a serial killer and we would never know?'

'Well, now it is . . .'

In essence, public transport is just a variety of different metal boxes on wheels that hurl you at your destination with little to no regard for your own personal space and with the added ingredient of people. And, as I've said before, people are awful. When trying to pinpoint exactly what it is I hate about public transport, and why it causes me to have so many panic attacks, it's hard to come to a conclusion. It's a mixture of social anxiety and being thrown into a situation over which I have no control. It's the complete absence of comfort zones: forced interaction with people (whether that's handing over a ticket or saying 'Excuse me' as you try to clamber your way through the train carriage); the confined space and no visible escape routes; the feeling that your carefully planned routine is now in the hands of someone else. You are essentially helpless.

I've had more anxiety and panic attacks on trains, in train stations and in airports than anywhere else. I can trace this back to when I was a child and the thought of going to an airport or on a long car journey would make me feel physically ill. I'm pretty sure the anxious population should get little badges like pregnant women get on the London Underground. But instead of 'Baby on board' it would say, 'I'm having a pretty tough time of it right now, please be nice to me' or 'This whole experience makes me very uncomfortable'. The end goal wouldn't be getting a seat, it would simply be people making room for us or, really, just not making eye contact with us. Public transport should be treated like a hospital waiting room: no one speaks to each other, we all have our own shit to worry about here, let's just get this over with as quickly and as painlessly as possible. But this would be too easy. Some people feel the bizarre need to interact with you, because some people have no personal boundaries. Say it with me: people are just awful.

There can be a very fine line between paranoia and anxiety at times. For instance, if someone was to catch my eye on the tube, my first thought would be, 'Oh God, why are they looking at me, I must have something on my face. Toothpaste? Dirt? Maybe they just think I have a really weird face. Do I have a really weird face?' Of course the rational response would be to assume it was a mistake on their part, but an anxious mess such as myself instantly assumes another human being is judging me, and in this case, solely on my appearance. How are you supposed to react to this sort of interaction? The British way is to simply look away, but then you run the risk of catching someone else's eye. There is an unspoken rule of public transport – stare at your phone and don't interact with anyone else

– but it is blatantly ignored by a large proportion of the population. Incidentally, I have been kept awake many times thinking about a similar event on the tube in which the man sat opposite made eye contact with me, and I winked. I WINKED. Why would I wink? What kind of normal person winks at someone? Only people in 80s sitcoms wink at each other. He did not wink back. I got off the train at the next station and waited for the next train to come along as I couldn't possibly travel with him for the rest of my journey. The humiliation was all-encompassing.

The anxious brain is extremely good at reading people and, at the exact same time, fucking terrible at reading people. Marvellous, isn't it? Our anxiety analyses the space around us – in this example, a rammed tube car – and instantly tries to identify who is a threat. Not in a *Daily-Mail*-esque 'Oh hey that guy has a tan I bet he's trouble' way, but in a 'That guy is being loud and talking to people and oh God wait he's coming this way holy shit he better not speak to me or I'll just have to . . . probably stand awkwardly and not say anything because my own safety is more important than vocalising my disdain at this talkative train menace' way. But while the anxious brain can go around a tube car and invent a negative backstory for every person within ten feet, the anxious brain is also particularly inept at reading people it has known for some time. You can sit next to your friend who you have known for sixteen years, enjoying a bottle of wine and watching a bad 90s movie, and while the other person is more than likely entirely content, in your own mind you are screaming: 'They are so bored, look at them, they hate you, they want to leave as quickly as humanly possible! How could they do this to us? I thought we were friends!' Rational. Completely rational. Even in the most comfortable of spaces, with people who are themselves part of your safety blanket, the anxiety-riddled mind never stops.

Every anxious person approaches situations in their own, unique, structured way. The problem with commuting is that you are thrown in with a group of people who have their own structures for this routine. And none of their routines agree with yours. My routine for commuting, which I do for two hours a day so I should probably get endorsed on LinkedIn for this, is as follows: bag on floor between feet so as not to obstruct anyone behind me, headphones on, book in hands, keep to self, don't fall over. It's an easy plan and it inflicts little to no impact on any of my fellow commuters. Other people though, other people have very little regard for anyone else's routines. They keep the keyboard clicks on their phones, the sound of which drills into your soul like the tapping of a furious robotic woodpecker. They play music from their phones out loud, and the people who do this usually play music that sounds like a ketamine-addled horse with a head injury causing a disturbance in a typewriter factory. They eat food that smells like it was left behind a radiator in a morgue for six years. They laugh out loud, to let all other passengers know they are having a better time than you, and their laughs are like a pig being thrown down stairs. It's a cavalcade of the worst traits in people, and you can't escape; there will be no reprieve, only keyboard clicks and the cruel honking of pig people.

A QUICK TOP TEN LIST OF THE WORST TRAIN PEOPLE YOU CAN ENCOUNTER:

10. Loud groups somehow having an amazing time on public transport
9. The man with no awareness for others trying to scream a conversation into a phone
8. The crying baby who is crying because, look, we all want to be crying but only this guy gets to do it in public
7. Man-spreaders
6. The loud chewer
5. The loud chewer who is eating food that smells like a horse died in a fart explosion
4. The lady who has left her keyboard clicks on to torture others
3. The man who STARES AT YOU for NO REASON (do not wink at him)
2. The young man listening to music from his tiny phone speakers in an attempt to somehow display dominance
1. The people who think the armrest is all theirs and so ELBOW WARS begin

'If this train was to catch fire how would we get out?'

'What kind of question is that?!'

'Well, we can't get to the exits because apparently six million people are in this carriage, that guy over there is blocking the only door with a suitcase the size of an Easter Island head and the woman next to you is standing on your bag.'

'This does seem like a less than ideal scenario. Any chance we can stop over-thinking this?'

'Of course not.'

The preferred ways to travel for the anxious brain, in numeric order:

1. Boat
2. Walking
3. Taxi
4. Train
5. Bus
6. Plane

Boat is only first because the number of times I require the use of a boat are minimal and I can't imagine many people boat their way to work on a regular basis. Unless you work on a boat. But then you still wouldn't commute to work on a boat. I don't think I know enough about boats to continue this train of thought any further. However, boats are obviously still terrible, like all transport, but they are the least terrible because of how infrequently I have to use them. The only times

I have to use a boat is when I visit my parents, who for some reason now live on a Scottish island, but the boat has a bar so I can self-medicate with nice whisky, a practice that is frowned upon on other forms of transport, most notably the 27 bus from Camden at 9 a.m. Once again, people are prudes.

Walking is the ideal scenario. If this can be planned out correctly the timings can always be pre-empted. You simply follow Google Maps, holding your phone before you like some sort of talisman in an Indiana Jones film, before wandering blindly into the distance. Actually a more accurate metaphor would be that thing they use in *Alien* that beeps when a xenomorph is arsing around in the vents, but that's terrifying. When you're walking the variables are all under your control. You can avoid people, you can go at your own pace, it is one of those very rare scenarios in which you can analyse and consider all the outcomes in a rational manner. However, it does come with its own risks, as every mode of transport does. You could get dive-bombed by pigeons at any given moment, or stabbed. Not by pigeons, pigeons don't have the correct hands to stab you with. At least I don't think so anyway, I'm not a pigeon expert. If I could I would walk everywhere, but I am also quite lazy and London is very big. Which is why walking isn't first on the list. Apathy wins again.

Taxis and Ubers are usually the preferred method of transport for the anxious human. They can fall in line with your rules, they can be scheduled and tailored to your lifestyle and, while you are trapped in a small space with a total stranger, if you begin to feel uncertain about your choice of travel, you can exit at your own will. The drawbacks here however are obvious. First, taxis are really expensive. Second, the drivers usually want to speak to you. Getting into a conversation with a taxi driver is second on the awkward anxiety scale only to having your hairdresser talk at you. Humans with anxiety are usually introverts, so their already prevalent social apprehension is multiplied when you hear a stranger say, 'So . . . going anywhere nice on holiday this year?' There are a limited number of conversations you can start with a complete stranger. The subjects usually involve: work, holidays, family, plans for the weekend and that's it. And all of these topics usually result in a one-sentence reply. Introverts don't do small talk. In fact this may be another occasion where our tube badges would come in handy again: 'I am very socially awkward, conversations cause me great internal pain'. I'm not entirely sure that would fit on a tiny badge but hey, I'm trying here.

Once again this awkwardness can be perceived as rudeness by those unfamiliar with anxiety or introverts, but it is the complete opposite. It is the complete fear of embarrassing oneself, or coming across as boring, uninteresting or in fact rude. Some people thrive on small talk, while others simply cannot bring themselves to partake in it. 'Why do you want to know about my weekend? You can't come. How will this influence your life? Will the knowledge of my weekend activities further your journey on this planet? Oh, you're just trying to be nice? Why? What do you want from me?' It's another in a long line of completely sensible ways to handle otherwise perfectly normal human interactions.

Trains take your routine and throw it away. Actually they don't just throw it away, they crumple it up, eat a little bit of it, then throw it away, into a bin, which is on fire. There should be an *X-Factor*-style competition on television, but instead of singing the contestants simply have to catch a train at a designated time from a regional UK train station. The show would last thirty years as the contestants all give up and/or die of old age. The timetable is subject to change, your seats are likely to change, your entire journey is subject to random cancellation. For anyone who needs certainty, this is not a good way to travel, and that's before you even consider the human element. But we've been over that (summary: humans are terrible). Most train companies advertise and pride themselves on the relaxing journey you get when you book with them, but nine times out of ten this couldn't be further from the truth. You are given, on average, three minutes from the time your platform is announced on the board to run to your platform, board your train, delve through the mass of confused passengers, stow your luggage away in a tiny compartment that is meant to fit one suitcase but which due to human perseverance is now filled with sixteen suitcases and find your reserved seat. Then the calamity of the reserved seat begins. If you were in a rush and couldn't book a reserved seat, you are now in an unconscious war with the other passengers to try to get a seat, which most of us will go to extreme lengths to obtain. Boarding a train can be more stressful than a round of the Crystal Maze, with the only reward being bad coffee and the occasional strange person touching your leg underneath the table.

Buses have only one thing going for them: if you begin to feel anxious or worried that you are out of your comfort zone, you can press a little red button and get off at the next stop. You have your escape route. They do however play by the same rules of uncertainty as trains because they can turn up whenever they want. Plus the driver may not even stop for you if they've had a bad morning and want you to suffer with them. Similar to trains, you are trapped in a metal box filled with people who unfortunately do not have the ability to give anyone personal space. And again, we have the whole experiencing-other-people thing. Many years ago I was catching a night bus home from a late shift at work. It was around 2 a.m. and the night bus was filled with people who looked like extras in a Mad Max movie. I sat in an available seat on the upper deck, with an empty seat next to me. As the bus got more and more full my seat remained empty. Every other seat was taken. People were standing instead of sitting next to me. This led to a conversation between my brain and me: 'OK, what's wrong with me? Why won't anyone sit next to me? Do I smell? Am I that repulsive? Oh God, do I look like someone who just rides the bus all night because I have nowhere else to go!?'

After several stops an old man sat next to me. At first I was relieved. And then . . . 'Good night?' he asked. I sat terrified. You can't speak to people on a night bus; that is destined to become a news story that ends with 'His body was found in the canal'. I was trapped in the taxi/hairdresser scenario all over again. He then produced a two-pint carton of milk. 'Have some,' he insisted. There are few things that I remember from school, but 'Don't talk to strangers' and 'Don't take bus milk from strangers' were definitely life lessons that I had internalised. It turned out it wasn't just milk: it was milk, Kahlua and vodka, essentially two pints of White Russian. It also turns out that an introvert with extremely low self-esteem, a strong desire to please others and an irrational fear of getting dumped in a canal is easily persuaded into drinking bus milk provided by a strange old man. If there is one lesson you take away from this book, it's that you should never let anyone manipulate your social awkwardness. And also never drink bus milk provided by strange old men*.

Anyway.

I fucking hate airports. Airports are chaos incarnate. There are no rules. It is every man for themselves. No one wants to be there. It is a means to an end. You want to go on holiday? You have to endure numerous hours of humanity at its very worst before you can get there. Social anxiety, separation anxiety, lack of comfort

---

* Side effects of bus milk include: nausea, night hallucinations, sweating, fear of bus milk and vomiting.

zones, a general theme of hectic uncertainty, you've got it all! It's your one-stop shop for an anxiety cocktail. I had the largest and most worrying anxiety attack I've ever had in an airport, but it was only years later that I would be able to identify it as such. You spend the day before getting ready to go there, you make sure your bags are the right weight, you check that you have your passport so many times that you actually increase the odds of you losing it by constantly faffing, you make sure that you have everything you need, that every possible scenario is taken care of. You wade through the crowds of panicked people, every single one of them terrified there will be one thing wrong with their passports or their luggage. You get to the check-in and you pray you've done everything OK so far. You go through security and you're almost positive you've done something wrong (even though at the same time you are fully aware you haven't); you are the person they always pat down and the person who always gets their luggage checked.

Then you proceed through duty-free, which is the single brightest place on the planet. White lights burn your eyes as you try to make your way through the bad perfume, the still-very-expensive cognac and the bizarrely large bars of Toblerone, and finally you get to a bar. Other people's tiny humans run around screaming due to boredom, people waiting for connecting flights lay themselves on any available floor space as if this was the safe zone after a zombie apocalypse. It's 10 a.m., you order yourself an alcoholic drink because this is an airport and time no longer makes sense and everything is awful. Then a metal cylinder filled with petrol flings you halfway across the world as you try to pack in as many free beers as you can. And this is all completely normal.

When I had that anxiety attack I didn't know what was happening. You know that red feeling you get in the back of your head when you're confused or furious? It was that, but it was all over my body and felt like it was taking over my entire being. The complete lack of control and the feeling of helplessness had turned my brain into – for lack of a better term – a madman's thinking porridge. The panic was everything, it was all I could feel. I became irrational and fearful of everything. This was before I knew that controlling my breathing and taking myself out of the situation would calm me down, so I simply embraced it. I embraced the confusion and the anger, because this is what my brain wanted me to do. The dangers that my brain construed as threats were completely nonsensical, but in that moment everything made perfect sense. I needed to panic, every part of me agreed that illogical rationalism was the only means of escape. Through the immense power of hindsight I can now tell that this all derived from a huge feeling of apprehension, but without the knowledge of what was happening, I was helpless.

Throwing yourself into this chaos of travel is troublesome for anxiety sufferers. It's against all our natural instincts to forcefully put ourselves into situations that our brains deem dangerous. The adrenal medulla (the part of the brain that deals with the fight or flight response) tells hormones to go bananas in your body in a misguided attempt to help you deal with the situation you have put yourself in. The anxious brain feels as if it should make you run, avoid these scenarios at all costs, but as a human being who observes other people completing these tasks with ease, you force yourself into it. You have to. It's the only way to make your life work properly, even if it does scare the living shit out of you.

One of the hardest things to do when your brain is your biggest enemy is argue with it. When all of your instincts are telling you to do one thing (be that run, flee or just crumple into yourself), you have to learn to fight it. In evolutionary terms this would have been where the caveman sees a bear for the first time, and his first response is to run, but upon further evaluation of the situation he decides to fight the bear, and then after they've put their differences aside they become best friends for ever and solve crimes.

I have no shame in equating coming face to face with a bear to getting on a rush hour train. It is yet another example of how your brain chemistry is against you. You should never feel guilty or ashamed that your brain is doing this to you. It doesn't make you any less of a person. The anxious brain wants you to feel bad, to feel worthless, and the best you can do is scream 'NOT TODAY, SATAN' and stand on that rush hour train. And even if you feel like you might perish at any moment, you have overcome something, you have dealt with a problem your brain wanted to flee from and you have kicked it into submission. And that's awesome. This is the root of exposure therapy; every time you fight against your irrational instincts your brain rewires itself, updating its firmware to adapt to this new revelation. We panic, we fight, we endure, we learn and we adapt, because we are brilliant.

TIPS FOR THE ANXIOUS TRAVELLER:

⚡ **Proper preparation.** Know where you are going and go earlier than you need to just in case anything goes wrong. Plan different routes just in case and have backup plans – you probably won't need them but in the back of your mind you'll feel calmer for having a plan B.

⚡ **Distractions.** Pack anything that can take your mind to a different place: books, portable games consoles, stupid little apps on your phone that involve moving one cube from that bit to that other bit – anything that can cause a little bit of escapism for your weary noggin. (If you're going on holiday take a Kindle. I once went abroad with seventeen real books and almost died carrying my backpack through the airport.)

⚡ **Treatlets.** What can work, even if it may seem a little silly, is taking a little bag of 'anxiety treats'. A ziplock bag to keep in your cabin bag that contains things to distract you on the journey. A small notepad and pen in case you want to keep an 'anxiety log' of how you are doing every fifteen minutes during your journey, no YOU'RE obsessive. Some sweets (or, for you Americans, candies) to keep your blood sugar high, a stress ball or something similar to keep your fingers busy. It can be whatever you need, just keep them close.

⚡ **Exercises.** These can be simple breathing exercises (in for four, pause for two, out for four) done quietly – you don't want people to think you're going into labour as this could result in people bringing you towels and hot water against your will. Raising one foot off the ground and turning it in circular motions to give you something to concentrate on, rolling your neck, tapping your index finger to your thumb in successions of four: any exercise you can find that helps you keep your mind in your current situation without it overloading. One of my favourites, which is incidentally from the movie *Die Hard,* is that when you are on a flight and you feel anxious, you should make fists with your feet. I don't know why it works, but if it's good enough for John McClane it's good enough for me.

5.
MY ANXIOUS BRAIN VS. WORK

(AKA Pirates, Bumbaclarts and Liza Minnelli)

In my opinion, there are three stages of human existence:

1. Birth.
2. The middle bit. A prolonged period of confusion, where nothing makes sense and everything is slightly terrifying. Occasionally you will meet people, which is also terrifying, and then – if you want to – you make tiny versions of yourself and that's also terrifying.
3. Death.

In the second part you have to do a lot of things that you don't want to do: go to school, shower, vote, eat salads, pretend to like sprouts at Christmas because you're BRITISH DAMMIT, oh, and work. Ah look, a handy segue into this next chapter!

The general problem here is you have to work to live. This is just one of those really boring facts of life that is tremendously difficult to argue with. There are some exceptions: you can win the lottery, or be the child of multimillionaires, or get hit by an ambulance and sue someone, but these are rare and usually you don't get this lucky in life. (Getting hit by an ambulance isn't lucky by the way, do not go out and get hit by an ambulance, they have more pressing things to do than to run you over.) If you want to live, you have to work. You have to make money so you can eat, so you can remain alive to go to work, so you can make money, so you can eat, and on and on and on and then you die. Disclaimer: at no point did I say this book would be inspirational.

There are very few professions suited to the anxious brain, but the ones I can think of are:

⚡ Professional cake tester where the cake is delivered to your house by drone.

⚡ Dog hugger, cuddler and general dog faffer-abouter where the dog is delivered to your house by drone (please do not attach your dog to a drone).

⚡ Pirate. Pirates always seemed pretty chilled out and you get a free parrot.

⚡ A job where you have to test which cushions are the best for finding a comfy position to read a book in.

⚡ Being the person who sees if drinking too much of one wine makes you blind or not.

⚡ Actually, I forgot that pirates got scurvy and avoided the law and that seems pretty stressful.

⚡ Cake tester and part-time dog faffer-abouter basically and probably drone repair-person.

Unfortunately a lot of these are completely unrealistic and life is in fact a cruel grind in which very few of us fall into the careers we really want to follow. Most people want to be a spy, or an astronaut, or a spy astronaut who gets paid in chocolate and hand jobs. But the real world is very different, and you generally have to settle for a vocation that six-year-old you would happily punch you in the tits for even considering. The way your teachers tell you life is going to work out is usually very different from reality. You don't get to achieve anything you can dream of, you get to achieve what society has available for you at that time. Like I said, this book isn't designed to be inspirational, but to help you find your own way, whatever that may be.

'Today is the day!'
'What day?'
'The day they all figure out we have no idea what we are doing.'

'We did OK on the last thing, I think we are in the clear. Also, fuck you I totally know what I am doing.'

'In the last meeting you didn't listen to a word anyone said and just doodled pictures of dragons.'

'Shut up.'

'You are in a meeting right now.'

'Your point being?'

'What are they talking about?'

'. . . things'

'You haven't got a clue have you? How are you a functional human being?'

'I DON'T KNOW.'

Welcome back our old friend imposter syndrome. The inescapable feeling that you do not belong. You could have worked your hardest, put your blood, sweat and tears into getting where you are today and still feel like at any moment the rug will be pulled from beneath your feet when everyone realises the failure you really are. With anxiety you worry, and even when you've put your most into this world, you will still worry, because anxiety is stupid and hateful. You worry that you're not doing well enough, you worry that your colleagues don't like you, you worry your boss thinks your work is fucking awful, you worry about talking to people, you worry about the commute, you worry and you worry and worrying is fucking exhausting. This all happens before you have even started work that day. This is the pre-game: inescapable fear, irrational dread, complete implosion of self-confidence, and you're only halfway through pouring your first coffee.

It's no wonder that anxiety sufferers don't hold themselves in high regard. Ego and anxiety rarely go hand in hand; people don't seem to be completely obsessed with themselves when they hate every part of themselves too. Personally I think this is what makes most sufferers better people to know. As you struggle endlessly with your own humanity and sanity, you rarely get time to forge an ego, claim self-importance, or mould some form of outlandish faux persona. The anxious brain tends to lean towards being humble, unable to take compliments, apologising constantly and not bragging when you achieve. It's another symptom of the disorder, but not necessarily a bad one, at least for other people. This sense of moral grounding can take years to achieve, and does not come naturally to many. So at least we have that! New anxiety symptom: violent politeness. (Anxiety: 6,000, Us: 1.) But when every job ad says, 'Confident person with outgoing personality who enjoys working in a team' it doesn't apply to many in our little bracket. If job ads said 'Shy person with good personality but isn't very good at showing it and works well with others as long as they don't expect any form of conversation' we'd be sorted.

FIVE WAYS TO MAKE WORK MORE BEARABLE:

1. Have someone you can talk to

This doesn't need to be someone in the office. If everyone you work with is a complete arsehole, then you don't want to divulge the innermost workings of your anxiety-ridden mind box to them. Send a friend a message, send a loved one a message – giving yourself a brief few seconds of escapism by focusing your energy on a constant that exists outside of work can be a great way of keeping you grounded. If the first two options aren't available, simply speak to people on your social media, there will always be someone to reply.

2. Lay off the caffeine

Yes coffee is awesome, but when you're seven coffees in, it's only 10 a.m. and you're screaming at Mike from Accounts, whose T-shirt is now strobing and giving you a headache, it's obvious that you need a new vice. All caffeine does is fuel whatever state of mind you are in at the moment, so if you're already anxious, now you're just really fast and anxious. If you're depressed, now you're just really fast and depressed. Try herbal teas, water, squash, or even just fruit – I know it sounds terribly healthy but it actually works.

3. Get out of the office (basically get away from work or real life)

Do it. Get the hell out of there. Go for a walk or something and just get your brain out of that space. It sounds obvious and I don't wish to patronise anyone reading this, but this is one that genuinely helps me on a day-to-day basis. Put your headphones on, listen to a good podcast or a playlist and even just a twenty-minute walk, or a walk to a park and then chilling out on a bench, will give your brain enough time to do a little reset. It's the closest I've come to 'turn it off and back on again' during a work day.

4. Drink plenty of water
Every book on mental health ever written will tell you to drink plenty of water throughout your day. It's either something to do with dehydration being linked to poor mental health or the mental health illuminati have stocks in the water industry and I've just stumbled upon one of the biggest conspiracies of our time.

5. Kill everyone in your office
It may seem a little extreme, but I recently watched a marvellous documentary called Falling Down where a man does this and it seemed to work out pretty well for him, I haven't seen the end though so don't spoil it.*

Of course, if all these highly scientific coping mechanisms aren't cutting it it's important to remember there is another option. If life is getting too much and your mental health has started to affect your work, or your work has started to affect your mental health, take time

---

* I'm kidding, obviously, no lawsuits please.

off. It's bizarre that in a society that is starting to take mental health problems more seriously we still refuse to take time off work to look after ourselves for non-physical illnesses. You wouldn't hesitate to take time off if your face was dripping with flu juice, but when your mind is exploding like a hamster in a microwave you just endure. It can seem overwhelming to talk honestly about your headtank with a boss or superior,* but you wouldn't have an issue if the illness was visible, you wouldn't hesitate if your arm had fallen off, you'd just say, 'Hello, my arm has fallen off, I think I should go home.'† Since the Equality Act of 2010 employers are legally required to not discriminate against employees suffering with mental health problems, if you do find yourself nervous about bringing up your issues with your boss, remember that the law is on your side.

There are many things about the workplace that can trigger the anxious brain: the size of a workspace, be it too small or too big (agoraphobia and claustrophobia); the forced interaction with other human beings (glossophobia); the bright lights (photophobia); the busy atmosphere (enochlophobia); the pressure of deadlines (deadlinephobia . . .?) (I've grown bored of listing

---

* Another option is that you can take a mental health sick day, which may involve lying and saying you're physically ill, but is a proven (if not temporary) technique.

† The fact that most men would probably go home rather than to the hospital if this happened is probably the subject of another book to be honest.

the technical phobia names now), the pressure of goals, the fear of humiliation, the terror of making a mistake. Things that 'normal' people find just a tad inconvenient send us weirdos into meltdown. (You're not a weirdo by the way, I was being massively flippant because deflection is my coping mechanism.)

(Unless you want to start a gang with me where we are called The Weirdos and get sweet leather jackets and go around singing like the gangs in *West Side Story*. I am being completely serious, I'm so up for this. Tweet me, let's talk jacket colour-schemes.)

(Sorry about that, my train of thought has become a nonsensical series of parentheses.)

With so many triggers it's easy to see how the anxious among us can encounter problems in the working world. However, with so little understanding of anxiety disorders, those who do suffer are usually referred to as 'the quiet one' or 'the weird one'. People are quick to judge. It's not a normal human reaction to look at a person and then spend some time analysing their personality before reaching a conclusion about them. Instead we typically take less than three seconds and have then formed an opinion that lasts the rest of our lives, because humans are stubborn and also mostly bastards. OK, it's half down to people being bastards, it's half down to this being yet another defence mechanism the brain uses to protect us. If we meet someone who we perceive as a negative human, we disapprove of them, as we don't need that extra pressure in our lives. On the other hand, when you observe a person with anxiety it can, as I said before, be perceived as rudeness, or shyness, or even arrogance. The physical ways in which anxiety manifests itself are very similar to negative qualities associated with people we avoid: sweating, shaking, stuttering, panicking, blushing, burping, overemotionality, all of which are completely involuntary, all of which are a complete pain in the arse. It's all stigma.

'Everyone here hates you.'

'OK WHY would you say that?'

'Just look at them, no one has said anything to you in hours.'

'That's because everyone is working . . .'

'No, it's because they hate you.'

'I'm trying to work, I don't need this.'

'See that guy?'

'Yes.'

'He hates you!'

'I'm going to ignore you . . .'

'See that woman?'

'Yes.'

'She hates you *and* she thinks you're ugly!'

'How is this helping?'

'At no point was helping ever in this agreement.'

'There was never an agreement here!'

'See that guy over there?'

And so on . . .

To steal an adage from *Star Wars*, where 'fear leads to anger, anger leads to hate' etc., anxiety leads to inner negativity, negativity leads to low self-confidence and low self-confidence leads to uncertainty and, not to repeat myself too much, but any level of uncertainty is an unwanted thing to the anxious mind. When you're constantly second-guessing yourself, and convincing yourself that every scenario is the worst one, coming across as someone who knows what they are talking about is extremely strenuous. Confidence is a gift that very few anxious people acquire and faking confidence is a skill that takes years to perfect. For example, the first time I had to lead a meeting with an important client I was sweating so much I looked like I had just run a 10K in an ill-fitting shirt. I stood in front of ten people, all of whom were terribly important suit-wearing folk, and attempted to discuss a new marketing strategy for their company. I had imagined that I would walk confidently into the office, blow them all away with my buzzwords and business know-how, receive a standing ovation at the end of the meeting and then be promoted or, at the very least, taken to a private cigar club and given a new cool nickname. The reality was quite different. I stood in front of those people, who controlled money that my company would hope-fully receive, and pretty much screamed at them for three minutes. I don't know why. I panicked. I had an out of body experience. I could see myself ruining everything but I couldn't stop myself (this is also a common theme in my life). I sweated so profusely that I had to dab myself down with a handkerchief like a villain in a western. I forgot the German word 'umlaut' and just shouted 'bumbaclart' for some reason. I started to hyperventilate and at times I would just let out a high-pitched cackle. I genuinely looked like I was having a breakdown that was written for a bad American sitcom. When I finished, I slumped into a chair and refused to make eye contact with anyone in the room. If I hadn't just sweated out 90% of my bodily fluids I would have run for the exit. A voice from the other side of the desk piped up, 'I think we have some good ideas here, and it's an umlaut not a bumbaclart but let's continue . . .' and everyone laughed. I remained dangerously dehydrated.

The one thing I take away from this story, which I do sometimes reinvestigate in the middle of the night, is that however you envisage an event going in your mind, it is either a best-case or a worst-case scenario. Your brain doesn't have time to deal with the numerous possibilities that lie between those points, so you get the best and the worst, and 99% of the time it's neither of these. You may not get your best-case scenario, but you're sure as hell not going to experience your worst either. For example, the next meeting I conducted at the same venue as above went fine. Not great, but at no point did I sweat so much you could see my nipples through my shirt, or want to vomit on anyone, so I'm counting it as a win.

Anxiety can border on paranoia: at times you can feel like you're losing your mind because it always jumps to the worst conclusions. But it's simply another evolutionary modification gone wrong. A mind predisposed to worry can easily fall into this trap; it's that pesky flight part of fight or flight again. The single worst piece of advice I ever received was from someone who said I worried too much, and their advice was: 'Stop worrying! Relax!' Reader, I was instantly cured. I went from nervous wreck to a fucking Buddhist.* Telling an anxious person to chill out is like telling a manic-depressive to cheer up, or telling a person with two broken legs to walk it off, or telling a dog in a tennis ball factory to calm the fuck down. It highlights a social ignorance that only serves to reaffirm to the sufferer that they are unable to switch emotions like a 'normal' person. So whether you suffer from anxiety yourself or know someone who does, just follow this one simple rule: don't be a dick.

HOW TO BE AROUND PEOPLE WITH ANXIETY:

⚡ Be a nice ordinary human being.

⚡ Repeat step 1.

⚡ Also, avoid asking too many questions. 'Are you OK?', 'You seem really quiet are you OK?', 'Are you not having fun?', 'Is there anything I can do?' can all seem like completely reasonable and polite enquiries, but more likely than not the person is fine,

---

* Is the sarcasm coming through here? I can't tell. It's difficult to emphasise sarcasm without changing the font entirely.

enjoying themselves, and this line of questioning is making them feel more on edge than they were previously. Simply say, 'If there is anything I can do let me know' and leave it at that. They then know that you are there for them and you have given them a safety blanket they didn't previously know that they had.

The anxious brain is prone to bouts of fixated perfection. You can see how you want something to work out and will work tirelessly to achieve this. On the other hand the anxious mind is also prone to bouts of apathy, where it's easier to simply ignore the task at hand, as that way it cannot be a source of stress. This usually results in worrying about the fact that you aren't worrying, which makes no sense but this is anxiety we are talking about here and nothing really makes sense. Procrastination is at one end of the scale and full, complete immersion is at the other end.

This is where we meet addictive personality disorder again. The need to prove yourself and the desire to do work so that no one is disappointed in you can result in you becoming a workaholic, which is akin to alcoholism in terms of ignoring reality. This may seem like an exaggeration, but the brain is particularly good at finding ways to fall into a circle of escapism. Escapism is the brain's way of tricking itself that the real world doesn't exist, that real problems are inconsequential, and for people struggling with even the smallest problems on a day-to-day basis, this is ideal. So after being given a sense of purpose and worth in any situation, the anxious mind can dive in head first and this can be perceived as the be all and end all, the only thing that gives you value. Work can be the root cause of anxiety for a lot of people. No one should treat their job as the only defining aspect of their personality, but when you have to work to acquire money, which then powers every other aspect of your life, it's easy to see why some can let it become all-encompassing. However, if your job is the main reason you are suffering with anxiety, then – and I don't say this lightly – you need a new job. There is no job in the world that should cost you your mental health. Of course that sentiment is an oversimplification; it is very unlikely that your job will be the sole reason for your mental health problems. However, if your job is a trigger then something has to change, be it with the way you approach your work, or sodding off from your job entirely and becoming a forest person who sells spells for food. That's your choice though, I am not legally responsible for anyone who has read this book who becomes a forest person.

Anyway. Your mental health is the one thing in life you are allowed to be entirely selfish over and if you can identify a trigger, or a cause of mental health problems, then you need to change it. Change is scary, and the enemy of routine, but can be one of the best things you could ever do. If you can identify any aspect of your day-to-day that only influences your life in a negative way then you are allowed to get rid of it.

For example, I have taken measures to cut negative people – people whose presence in my life had no positive influence on me – out of my life. It's difficult, but you feel a bit new afterwards. It's the human equivalent of making some spare room on your hard drive by deleting some of those old photos you don't look at any more; afterwards things just run a little bit smoother.

As one of the great philosophical thinkers of our time, Liza Minnelli, once said, 'money makes the world go around'. The anti-establishment 70s movement known as ABBA said 'money, money, money', and one of the great poets of the 90s, Mr Notorious B.I.G., said 'Mo' Money, Mo' Problems'. Financial anxiety is a weight that everyone has felt at some point. A weight that sits on that annoying bit of your neck just by your shoulders, making you hunch and feel low. You can see people walking around without this weight; they can buy things, sure, they can go to the pub every night, they can buy new shoes because they fancy it and not because their old pair fell apart on the bus to work . . . but everyone worries about money. Everyone.* It is a universal truth, and it is a rational and calculated threat to let your brain worry about. But as ever, anxiety takes the volume control on worry and ramps it up to 11.

---

* Maybe not extremely rich people, the kind of people who can afford a swimming pool filled with dildos or Tesco Finest lasagnes.

When I started writing this book I realised that to properly get an idea of how anxiety affected people I would need to speak to people with anxiety. My first thought on this was 'But I hate talking to people and actively avoid it at all points'; my second thought on this was 'But I hate talking to people and actively avoid it at all points'. After arguing with myself I sent out emails to people I knew who suffered with the condition, people whose writing on the subject had inspired me, people who had brains that worked like mine.

I ended up sitting in a small cafe in Greenwich with Daisy Buchanan, aforementioned author and journalist, who has spoken openly about her own battles with anxiety. Halfway through our coffees we started discussing financial anxiety:

'I have tons and tons of financial anxiety. I'm a freelancer, I can get obsessed with how much money I have coming in. I went through a phase of not checking my bank balance for three or four years, and I couldn't use cashpoints, I panicked that there wouldn't be any money in there, so I didn't look! I just waited for a phone call from the bank saying: "We've been meaning to call you, you're going to prison." A completely normal reaction to handling money, I know. Eventually I just had to look, I forced myself. I still hate it, I still think I am going to look one day and there won't be anything there, even if I've just been paid and I know that's impossible, I worry there won't be anything there, but I do check . . .'

It's understandable, the fear of checking your own financial accounts. Some even ignore their bills, instead hiding them under the sofa until the sofa is several feet taller than it used to be and is now in fact completely useless as a sofa. But while most of the time you know that you are fine, that one time you check and it's less than you thought, it's like having a machine in a wall telling you that you're a failure. Your paranoia about your own worth has been displayed right in front of your eyes in an obnoxious green font. We equate so much to our financial gains: our statuses can be defined by the contents of our wallets (take, for example, those Tinder profiles of men sitting on boats/sports cars), so of course the anxious mind would try to avoid any problem it identifies as a threat, and put off turning it into a reality for as long as it can.

Don't worry, I'm not going to give you financial advice here. Bloody hell, my bank balance often hovers at zero; but if there is one piece of advice to give in relation to financial anxiety it's this: do your best, whatever that is. Check your accounts when you can, save when you can. No one is good with money, apart from stockbrokers and those creepy men reclining on cars. Hell, we are now in an economy where it's going to take 700 years to save up for the deposit for a first house, so let's worry about that instead. Oh God now I am worrying about that. Shit.

The counterbalance to work life is a social life, which we will address in more detail in a later chapter because that's also completely horrible, but you need to be able to enjoy your time outside of work in order to function as a human being. The objective should be to take your mind off the day that you have just endured. Not to sound like a motivational quote that your auntie would share on Facebook, but you only get so much time to yourself, time that you own, time that you can control, time in which you can put your own selfish needs first. Don't get me wrong, this isn't one of those books in which I am going to advise you to light some incense, cross your legs and meditate to find your centre – you don't have time for that, you're knackered. But if you do have time, go for it, I'm not your mum.

I have been an adult for a fair amount of time now – apparently – and I feel that adulthood can be summed up thus: 'Being an adult is just feeling tired all the time and telling people you feel tired and then they reply saying that they are tired too.' I've found that the best way to succeed in putting your anxious mind to sleep is to fall victim to your own ideas. What will take your mind off work? Or off reality? Escapism. Ridiculous, delicious escapism. The majority of people with anxiety who I speak to say that switching off is the hardest part. Whatever you are doing that isn't productive feels like a waste of time. I have spoken to people who have voiced their disdain for sleep as it is a time in which so much more could be being achieved. But the fact is, if you don't switch off occasionally you are heading towards a breakdown. (All work and no play makes Jack more likely to suffer a mental breakdown that could result in chasing children through a maze with an axe.)*

The human mind can only take so much stimulus. If you exhaust your mind through work and responsibilities, it's the equivalent of having too many tabs open in an Internet browser: eventually the browser will crash. Every other week you hear about the rock star who toured too much and needed time off due to exhaustion or ended up in rehab because of their Furby addiction (that sounds stupid but rich people always get addicted to the weirdest things, like BDSM or slippers or something). Or the sports star who pushed too much and injured themselves. It's the same with mental health: if you take too much on, you will burn out. It's easy to find things to keep you preoccupied, it's just discovering what works for you. I don't mean to be patronising but you can always try cooking a meal for yourself, cleaning your flat, reading, writing, doing something creative, going for a walk, listening to music. It really is whatever you define downtime as. You don't have to become someone who climbs Mount Everest for fun or someone who becomes the next great artist; just do whatever you feel comfortable with, whatever puts your mind in

---

* *The Shining* is actually a film about the pressures of self-imposed over-expectation on the human brain and no one can tell me any different.

airplane mode, and go with it. Personally, I will be spending the next hour watching videos of dogs doing things dogs aren't supposed to do. For example, the dog in this first video is best friends with a parrot, and all is well with the world.

6.
A BEGINNER'S GUIDE TO ANXIETY, PART 2:

(AKA Well, it starts off with anxiety and then goes into mental health in general but I needed a snappy title for this chapter because as you can see, this as a title would be too long)

(Trigger warning: In this chapter I discuss self-harm and suicide. If you are not comfortable with these topics I will remind you further into the chapter so you can skip these bits.)

In chapter two I attempted to lay out a basic idea of how anxiety works, and drew on my own personal experiences to discuss anxieties that I had experienced and could discuss confidently. The psychological, the physiological and the sociological schools of thought around anxiety are vast, with thousands of definitions, thousands of types of therapy and an uncountable number of articles and works on the subject. Finding the diagnosis that works for you can be hard, and more often than not is a tiring mixture of trial and error and hurling yourself out of your comfort zone. We've briefly covered the evolutionary aspects of how our amygdala came to perceive the threats around us, and how bursts of neurotransmitters often work against us, so let's take a break from getting through our day-to-day and look in a bit more depth about why we actually feel like this, and reaffirm that we are not 'crazy' or 'mad' (even though I joke about these labels); we are just built a little differently.

I sat in a museum cafe in Euston, waiting to conduct another interview for this book. I am not one to romanticise what was in fact a pretty dreary coffee shop with a bookshop attached, I'm not going to bore you with the 'emotionless expressions on the patrons as they ordered watered-down coffee' or say how 'the flickering lights in the rafters were a metaphor for our twisted human souls engaging in mindless activities'; I will simply say, I people-watched. I had turned up forty-five minutes early to the meeting, as my own anxieties will not allow me to be late for appointments, so I was there ridiculously early to ensure that I was definitely there on time, and I'd sat in the emptiest area so as to avoid other people. Typical anxious behaviour. Some people can people-watch for hours – when my wife and I go on holiday, we sit in little bars, share a bottle of wine and people-watch, inventing backstories for all the strangers around us. (This is also a helpful tool if you are uncomfortable in a public place; humanising everyone around you takes the fear out of the situation.) As I sat in this cafe I simply thought how weird humans were. The human body is, for lack of a better metaphor, an elaborate transport mechanism for our brains. Everything we are, everything we define ourselves as, lives in a 1.3-kilogram squidgy flesh sponge* crammed into a skull helmet. Our brains are the pilot and our bodies are just clunky, clumsy vehicles for it.

I was meeting with Dean Burnett, a neuroscientist and author of *The Idiot Brain*. As I had already spoken to sufferers, I wanted a more clinical look at the condition and he had kindly agreed to meet me. I started with the same question I was asking every interviewee: 'How would you define anxiety?'

'[Anxiety] is a general unease, a constant apprehension that things are going to go badly. I mean it's quite difficult to define without using the word anxiety to be honest, but it really is a feeling of things going wrong. It doesn't tie to anything specific, it's not something that will ever go away, it is an evolutionary threat mechanism ingrained into our DNA.'

* Fun fact: you know those boxes of wine you can get that make drinking wine more enjoyable because of the cool little taps? Well, take the box off and hold the wine bladder (for want of a better expression) in your hands: that's how much a human brain weighs. Cool huh? Well *I* thought it was cool. I'm never telling you anything ever again.

My interviewing skills are not going to make me the new Louis Theroux or Jon Ronson. My interviewing style is 'blurt out questions really quickly and try not to show how intimidated you are by these clever people oh God don't fuck this up'. I asked Dean about the role of the amygdala and cortisol in our anxious brains; my knowledge until this point was 'The amygdala is a bit of a tit' and 'Cortisol can fuck off', so I felt like I needed a more intellectual look at this.

'Cortisol is our stress hormone, it's what gets us ready for our fight or flight response,' he explained. 'The amygdala is the threat centre of the brain; it's the main hub of a threat detection network that scans all the incoming information and looks for threats, like a security camera – it's constantly on the lookout for trouble. Threat detection doesn't do a great job of figuring out real threats compared to things we are expecting to happen. "There's a wolf coming towards me" – that's a threat, but "I might lose my job if the economy doesn't recover" – that may never happen. It's not a real physical thing, but it is still perceived as a threat and causes stress. The brain finds it difficult to find the difference between an imagined threat and a physical threat, to separate what is actually in front of us and what we have invented for ourselves. The amygdala triggers the fear response. Cortisol diminishes the flow of serotonin (a happy chemical), keeping us constantly on edge. Essentially it over-analyses; anything it can see as a threat it will stick with that.'

The term 'fight or flight' was coined by Walter Bradford Cannon, an American physiologist (hey look an actual fact in this book! See, learning can be fun!), who in 1915 was researching how animals reacted in times of stress. The example most commonly used for this is if a zebra is grazing peacefully, having his morning grass snackathon, and sees a lion busying about in the distance, the zebra thinks to himself 'Fuck this' and legs it. Obviously those aren't the words Dr Cannon would have used. The zebra's senses are heightened, its muscles tense and its blood is redirected to all the parts of the body needed to get it the heck out of there. Another example: your cat meets a dog or a bear or a cucumber or whatever cats are afraid of. It will tense up, the hairs on its back will stand on end. This isn't to make itself look big, it's to dissipate heat from the body so it can cool down and prepare to launch itself into the distance, usually taking out whatever expensive ornaments are around it at the same time. I told you learning was fun.

Later studies found that humans have a similar reaction. Our brain receives information, the amygdala checks to see if it's a threat or not, decides 'Oh this doesn't look great' and floods our bodies with cortisol and adrenaline.

THE PHYSICAL REACTIONS TO AN EVENT OF FIGHT OR FLIGHT ARE:

⚡ Sweating (cooling your body ready to escape)

⚡ Muscle tension (getting your limbs ready to leg it)

⚡ Quickening of your heartbeat (faster heart = faster movement and blood flow increases – this is also what causes blushing when you're anxious)

⚡ Shortening of breath (still getting you ready to leg it)

⚡ Going pale (blood leaving your skin and going to where it needs to be used)

⚡ Evacuation of the bowels (getting rid of excess weight)

Any of these sound familiar? This is just how our brains are wired, it is in our DNA, it's what has kept our species alive for so bloody long. But why do we perceive threats in social situations, busy elevators or stressful board meetings? Why do we react like a zebra about to get toothed to death when presented with an activity that most other humans find easy?

'I think a lot of it is just to do with the fact that the world is a safer place now,' Dean told me as I quaffed my third coffee in half an hour. 'Until last century life was pretty horrible anyway, you would work down the pits and die by age twenty-three – very real threats existed in day-to-day life. The body has just not adapted to a modern world. We live in a world where there are not as many physical threats, so we now worry about existential things, "I know I'm not going to get hit by a comet tomorrow, but what if?" and we make ourselves panic. Compared to a hundred years ago, we have more job security, better healthcare, our scope of things to worry about has gotten smaller – but our brains haven't caught up yet.'

Society has advanced more in the last fifty years than it had done in the previous several centuries, with the pace of life getting faster, constantly changing infrastructure and daily advancements in technology and the way we live our lives. We simply haven't had a chance to let our evolutionary defaults catch up with our modern existences. Let's put it another way: in the so-called 'good ol' days' our main worries were getting food for the family, keeping our heads down and meandering through life by keeping whatever cards it had given to us close to our chests. Now, with access to more information than ever before, with more expectations set upon us than ever before, we've learned to transpose our fears onto more metaphysical things. Not to disagree with Kierkegaard (why don't I just MARRY Kierkegaard?), but we are not so much living in an 'age of anxiety', we are living in an age of catastrophic thinking. People living in the western world are living with more stress today than in any other age, but that's not to say that world events are more stressful than ever before. There have been wars since men first thought 'Hey, fuck that guy', there have been outbreaks of disease in every civilisation, many different generations have experienced economic uncertainty, so what makes the current generation of humans so inclined to states of worry and feelings of unease? The answer may lie in the way we now perceive our world.

Let's get one thing straight before I get into this, I

am not about to demonise the Internet. As I said earlier, I think it can be a great space for support and expression. The world has always been a shitheap; adding phones into this has not created a generation of vacuous, self-absorbed technology zombies. People are people, people use the tools they have access to in order to further their education and skill, Tim Berners-Lee has not doomed us all to a dystopian future where the human race becomes enslaved by machines.* What has fundamentally changed is the way we receive information. Over the last 100 years our access to information has gone from being a knackered pigeon flying 400 miles to tell you your Great-aunt Bessie has dysentery to having access to the entirety of human knowledge in your pocket. Perhaps our brains weren't ready to comprehend so much information at once? Evolution takes thousands – hundreds of thousands – of years, and in less than 500 years we have completely changed the way we think about almost every situation. It's not irresponsible to think that maybe our brains are just trying to play catch-up with us here.

Catastrophic thinking is the idea that the human brain is predisposed to jumping to 'worst-case scenarios'. In the good ol' days, when everyone lived in tiny villages, 'Land of Hope and Glory' played on repeat in the background at all times and the most shocking event

---

* But if that future does come along and you're one of those people who says they won't have sex with a robot if that becomes a possibility, you're lying.

to befall us was a cow running into Mabel from church, our brains just thought 'OK this is pretty sweet'. Nowadays you turn on your TV and the news is just a long series of nightmares, you open your phone and every negative and disaster is beamed into your face through notifications. Terror attacks, overpopulation, economy crashes, dictators, weapons of mass destruction, Brexit, Trump. You usually feel relieved if a piece of news pops up in your life that doesn't have the fear of death looming over it. Everyone is scared all the time, we are all feeling helpless in this world, and what are we doing to combat it? Jumping to catastrophic conclusions whenever we can. It's your irrational brain defeating your rational brain again. The way we consume information and interpret it into real threats may explain why cases of anxiety have increased exponentially since the 1950s, with an entire industry of pharmaceutical companies making billions from the rise of medication culture.

There are schools of thought within the psychiatric community that hold that the decline in religious sentiment can be blamed for our increasing state of unease. Our ancestors were mad religious – all the art was about God or Mary or Buddha, all the music was about it, people were well up for a good religious figure – but today we are a bit more apathetic towards living our entire lives serving a 'higher power' on the off-chance an afterlife exists. Does a lack of religion make us worry more? Does the idea of comprehending our own insignificant mortality – instead of just thinking 'Oh well, at least I'm going to heaven!' – make us a bit more anxious? God knows. (See what I did there?)

As we've covered, the rapid advancement of society has done nothing to help our collective mind. If we think about how quickly our world has changed, it becomes a terrifying notion. For example, some molluscs found in Iceland were born before America was ever a thing. We live in a world where some sea creatures are older than the largest economy in the world, lucky bastards. Are molluscs born? Or are they hatched? Or just you know . . . created. Sorry, it's not time for a mollusc-related existential crisis. As Ferris Bueller says, 'Life goes pretty fast, if you don't stop and look around you might miss it.' We are now in an age when we are constantly trying to live our lives to the fullest! Climb every mountain! Experience all the experiences! We're just trying to justify our short time on this rock of weirdness, but in doing so we spend half our lives worrying about whether we are doing it right. We worry about 'could haves', we worry about 'what ifs?', we worry about every bloody thing.

Another argument within the scientific and psychological community is about the impact of genetics versus environmental influence on the prevalence of anxious disorders. Nature or nurture. I'll let Dean take the lead on this one:

'It's a combination of both. We are predisposed to register threats, it's part of our DNA. The tendency to over-think things is a genetic inclination, but an excess of over-thinking can be environmental; it can be a factor of our upbringing. There is evidence that you can inherit mental health disorders from your parents – schizophrenia and depression, for example. But being inclined to excessively worry can also be a case of imprinting behaviour. If you have an alcoholic parent you are more likely to become an alcoholic in later life because of the situations you were raised in. Your upbringing has a big influence on the way your brain develops, if you have an overly worried parent who overreacts to everything and you grow up with that behaviour around you, you will be influenced by this behaviour. There is a strong genetic element, but also a strong environmental element, it's difficult to split the two.'

While anxiety as a medical condition is genetic – an evolutionary whoopsie-daisy stitched into our DNA like a swear word sewn into a Christmas jumper – the way anxiety can play a part in our lives can be traced to the ways in which we were brought up, and the situations we encountered. A child's brain is like a sponge: useless, can't do advanced arithmetic, yellow . . . Hang on, where was I going with this? Ah yes, a child's brain is like a sponge: absorbing everything it comes across. The main hereditary argument for anxiety being passed down through generations is in the serotonin transfer gene – a chromosome that we all have, so if a parent is genetically predisposed to low levels of serotonin (our nice happy chemical) then this can be passed down through our genes at the most basic of levels. However, the schools of thought tend to lean towards upbringing and imprinting being a larger factor than genes. Let's use a nice over-worked metaphor for a change! There are two children: one was raised in an average home, average parents, average school etc.; the other was raised by survivalists in a bunker as their parents were terrified of a nuclear apocalypse and thought that the government were stealing their thoughts so dressed entirely in cling film and only spoke through a series of clicks and whistles. Which kid do you think will be more anxious in later life? Are they inheriting their parents' phobias and imbalances or is it being inflicted upon them? The major factors in being raised to be more susceptible to anxiety in later life are:

1. Your parents being terrified of most things in the world (catastrophic thinking)
2. Your parents putting too much pressure on you to perform well or being overly critical (leading to low self-esteem, low confidence, imposter syndrome)
3. A lack of emotional security (loneliness, improper emotional development) or too much emotional security (attachment figures and separation anxiety)

This isn't where I give parents tips on how to parent, that would be hypocritical and ridiculous, the main takeaway from this is the reflective way our brains receive stimuli from an early age. Remember all the stories we heard when we were young about babies being raised by wolves and then when they were rescued they still acted like wolves? That's because that's what the brain has observed and mirrored as a crucial part of development. I for one would like to see a child raised by ducks and see what they look like at five or six, or a child raised by sloths and see if the kid moves really slowly, and this my friends, is why I am not a scientist. (Or why I definitely SHOULD be a scientist, could go either way.)

GENDER

'Don't write about gender.'
'Why not?'
'You'll do something that will piss people off.'
'Almost definitely.'
'Don't do it then.'
'Hold my beer.'

As we carry on trundling our way through the world of anxiety, our next stop is the wonderful world of gender. Fifteen per cent of Americans and 18 per cent of us Brits will suffer with anxiety at some time in our lives but when it comes to gender, according to the DMSV, we get a nice even 2:1 split, with twice the number of women in the general population suffering from anxiety (and depression) than men. Anxiety has always been weirdly skewed to being a female condition, most commonly shown by being portrayed in films as 'female hysteria' e.g. the 'anxious friend' or the 'pill-popping mom'. As a society we lean more towards assuming women will have anxiety, while men are just 'having a hard time' or 'going through some things'. This is why so much advice around anxiety can be 'take a hot bath, imagine you're in a spa and do more women things like laugh at yoghurt'. So why is anxiety so associated with women? And are men, through their sheer brazen stubbornness, falling behind when diagnosed, or are we simply less anxious?

A Brief History of Antidepressants and Anti-anxiety medications

When we think of the good ol' days, what do we think of? Black and white images of housewives doting on a washing machine like it was a child, men in suits walking to work with a newspaper in one hand and a belt in the other because child abuse was still pretty OK at this time. Kids skating around wearing puffer jackets and trying to get back to 1985. It all seems quite romantic doesn't it? In 1955, a little pill called Miltown burst onto the American market, the first mass-manufactured anti-anxiety medication, and the first prescription medication to be as widely available as anti-anxiety meds are today. By 1963, one in twenty Americans were taking Miltown – or one of the similar drugs available; but Miltown was the one everyone wanted all up in their head factory. Hollywood parties incorporated it into their cocktails, with luxury brands even releasing limited edition pill cases. There was very little marketing for Miltown, with word of mouth playing a major part instead, and its nickname spread like a cold in a preschool: 'Mother's Little Helper'. One in twenty American women were now medicated up to their beehives. Was living during the Cold War the start of catastrophic thinking? Were all their minds focused on their children's new discovery of rock and roll, milkshakes and dancing the Mashed Potato, and was this a valid cause of concern? Or were serious cases of anxiety being overlooked in favour of a fashion statement in the form of pharmaceuticals, as the Hollywood elite stood at award ceremonies and implied that their success was due to their use of Miltown? Fuck knows frankly, but 'Big Pharma' was rolling in so much cash they could have done a Scrooge McDuck and dived into an Olympic swimming pool filled with dollars. The 70s saw the anxious self-medicate with weed.* Then in the 80s and 90s, America found itself in a love affair – maybe not a love affair, more of a dirty romp in a back alley – with Prozac and Valium. Unlike Miltown, these weren't gendered, they weren't 'Mother's Little Helper'; they were everyone's secret happy pill. But once again, the celebrities were on it, the bankers were on it, it was praised in the media and instead of being seen as a medicine that helped ill people, it was seen as a status symbol. Companies were making billions, prescriptions went through the roof, the western world was now happily chomping down antidepressants like a duck finding a loaf of unguarded Hovis.

* Here's a fun side note: if you are on tricyclic antidepressants, don't do weed. I spent an afternoon thinking I was melting.

Anyway, back to our regularly scheduled nonsense. The vastly different number of men, women and trans men and trans women* suffering with anxiety at a statistical level seems confusing when you boil it down to genetics. With all of our brains coming from the same biological and evolutionary beginnings, it must be more of a sociological element that adds fuel to the fire that is anxiety. In the trans community the largest factors for anxiety stem from coming out, or the process of transitioning. This is completely understandable, with society still not quite wrapping its head around the fact that (prepare yourselves, this next idea is pretty radical) human beings are just human beings regardless of how they identify. So the pressure on people of all ages as they transition is of course going to be a great source of anxiety and also depression. The more you stray from what society deems 'normal', the more your susceptibility to anxiety grows. Rates of anxiety differ when looking at sexuality as well. Within the lesbian, gay and bi community anxiety rates are at 20%,† a sharp increase on the 15% of the heterosexual population. As the world changes, as do our perceptions of gender, there is one group to blame for this: yes, feminists. Bloody feminists, with their calls for equality, equal pay, not to be harassed in the workplace, not to be judged on their bodies, not being happy to just shoot

---

* In the trans community, rates of anxiety jump to 33.2% of the population.

† http://www.apa.org/monitor/feb02/newdata.aspx

out babies like a potato gun and spend the rest of their days quaffing down Miltown and listening to Gary Barlow or whatever it is women do. It's almost like women want to be treated like real people? Bizarre. (I'm obviously joking, I like my women like I like my coffee, strong enough to kill me but with a hint of mercy.)

The sociologists Walter Gove and Jeannette Tudor argue that the rise in mental health problems in women stems from changing gender roles after World War Two. The housewife was not only left to look after the family, run the household and be a doting wife, but now also had financial responsibilities outside the house.

Another aspect that may contribute to the large gap between male and female mental health is our gendered idea of emotion. Women are seen as more emotional, hell, even the word 'hysteria' comes from the Greek for uterus: the Greeks, because they were all bananas, thought a woman's excessively emotional state was caused by a wandering uterus. Just where this uterus was wandering off to is still unknown. Men, on the other hand, are told from a young age to not show emotion, to 'man up' and get on with things. Maybe the discrepancy between genders and mental health is down to men ignoring their disorders, a sheer stubbornness to continue with things: to man up. Or maybe it is down to women being more open with their emotions. The psychologist Amanda Rose attributes this to what she calls 'co-rumination', which describes the sharing of negative feelings and exploring negative experiences with friends. We all know our closest friends are the ones we can share our deepest feelings with, and as women are more open to doing this than men, this may lead to more women getting help, while men are more unlikely to discuss emotions with each other, instead substituting these conversations for burping or pointing or comparing balls or something, I don't know.

Of course another explanation for this discrepancy is an obvious sociological issue: women just don't get treated the same as men do in society. As I say that I can hear the thunderous clacking of thousands of men's rights activists about to go 'WELL ACTUALLY' into their keyboards, but it's true. As gender roles have changed so have gender expectations: women are told to look a certain way, act a certain way, be a certain way, do everything correctly so you can shoot babies out of yourself like some sort of person cannon and have flawless make-up while you do it. If you put too much pressure on someone, they will crack, and if you put too much pressure on a gender, you see a sharp gender difference in the rates of mental health problems. When it boils down to the real *why* of trying to find out the big difference in the numbers, there isn't one definite answer. Some books say it's gender roles, others say it's lack of education, but all we know for certain is that regardless of gender, some human beings are struggling, and they need any help they can find.

Mansplaining

The one particular topic I have any real right to talk about with any sense of proficiency in this sub-chapter* is the rise of anxiety (and mental health problems in general) among men. I myself am a man, I have checked and everything, and I am a man with anxiety, so let's see how I can fuck this up.

Men live most of their lives under the weight of an imposed sense of masculinity. We are told to be tough, to be the hunter-gatherer, to be the hero, the bread-winner, the protector. Man up. Boys don't cry. In my not-so-professional opinion, this is a whole level of bollocks. The human brain does not consider your gender when it lambasts you with mental health disorders. A series of chemicals and neurotransmitters do not see 'blue is for boys, pink is for girls', these tiny biological processes inside of your head just see you for what you are, a human being. The sociological impact of a forced sense of masculinity and bravado has been bigger for both sexes than we could have ever imagined. You are not weak for thinking you need help, you are simply you, and you cannot help that.

Keeping things to yourself, never speaking of them, pretending that everything is fine, will be far more damaging than recognising them. This is the heart of the issue: many men do not feel comfortable discussing

---

* Fun fact: sub-chapters are usually only found in books about the Navy . . . Yes I know that is a terrible joke but I found it hilarious and I didn't want any of you to miss out on it.

their mental health with other men, or with anyone for that matter. It can still be seen as weak, some will see it as revealing fragility, and if you've lived most of your life fighting those notions to live a lie of bravado, that can be terrifying. It is my opinion that the rise in male mental health problems over the last decade isn't a sudden explosion of diagnoses and problems, but of men who are now brave enough to finally admit to themselves that they may need help. One person discussing their problems can inspire others to do the same; this is why representation is so bloody important. Men are stubborn, they will not easily give out personal information, but if we know that doing so can benefit us, that doing this can make our lives better and will not bring shame upon a thousand generations of our family, we may be more inclined to do so. The problems have always been there, we learn to live with them, we learn to ignore the voices in our heads telling us we are crazy, but as more people speak openly and honestly, more people will recognise themselves in those conversations, and will finally not feel so alone.

The gritty reality of unspoken male mental health issues is that when a human being is suffering in silence, their problems will manifest themselves in other extremely negative ways. Alcoholism, drug addiction and domestic violence are all unhealthy and destructive ways in which mental health problems present themselves. These mental health problems can be dealt with, they can be reasoned with, but after so many years of denial they show themselves in ways that ruin lives and destroy families, all because men are taught to be too proud to admit fault. The biggest killer of young men in the UK is suicide. It is now such a problem that most charities that work in this field would describe it as an epidemic. We have accidentally created a generation of men who feel so alone that they convince themselves that there is only one solution. But over the last decade we have seen many high-profile men speak openly about their own battles with their demons, including Prince Harry, Bruce Springsteen, Zayn Malik, Professor Green, Stephen Fry . . . men from different backgrounds with wildly different audiences, opening up about issues that not so long ago would have been easily dismissed or jeered at. If a single comment like the ones made by the men listed above can strike a chord with a man out there who is struggling, then it is worth it. We have to be there for each other, it is our duty. We have outlived the old notions of gender roles and ridiculous notions that boys don't cry, now we're finally getting to a place where we can say 'Boys do cry, and that's perfectly fucking normal.'

It is a universal duty to ignore the bizarrely gendered rhetoric of mental health problems: our brains are our brains, we are all human beings, we have emotions, we have good moments and bad moments, we are not infallible, we should never be too proud to ask for help. However, that is an idyllic notion that exists in my utopian fantasies. (In this utopian fantasy currency has been replaced with ice cream and everyone gets a dog on the NHS too, but moving on.)

As gender roles evolve, I hope that society too can evolve, letting a new generation of men know that it's perfectly fucking human to be in touch with your emotions, that suppressing your brain is never the right path, so let someone hold your hand. Personally, I think talking openly about your anxiety, about your depression, about whatever mental health problem plagues your noggin, can be one of the manliest things you can ever do. I've been there, I've been this low, I've hidden behind fake machismo, and it did more bad than it ever did good. Oh and while we are talking about the gritty and unpleasant side of mental health disorders . . .

THE DARK SIDE OF MENTAL HEALTH: LEAVE YOUR JOKES AT THE DOOR.

(Trigger warning: Yeah this is the bit I was talking about at the beginning of the chapter, skip this section and go to page 133 if conversations about self-harm or suicide make you uncomfortable or could trigger anything for you. Look after yourself by skipping this.)

As we've been going through this book you'll have noticed a slight and very subtle mocking tone when it comes to how I approach my anxiety and anxiety in general. I mock my anxiety because it gives me control over it. It is always with me, making my life more difficult than it needs to be, but if I can find the humour in it, I can make it seem smaller than it really is. But let's get serious here for a moment. (This is the bit where if it was a high school comedy and I was the cool substitute teacher who all the kids prefer to the actual teacher, I'd spin a chair around and sit on it backwards, because I don't play by the rules of this school.) Anxiety is a fuckwit, we all know this, and it can range from being a mild inconvenience to a destructive disorder that can ruin, and in some cases end, lives. Those with anxiety are more likely to attempt suicide than the rest of the population, those with anxiety are more likely to self-harm than the rest of the population. This is why it is so important that we look out for each other, that, as a community, we just ask each other, 'Are you okay?'

Self-harm isn't a laughing matter. It comes in many shapes and forms, from ripping the skin off your fingers, to pulling out your hair, to cutting yourself, to leading a self-destructive lifestyle. Self-harm is anything that an individual does to purposefully endanger themselves. The main reason people self-harm is for that momentary distraction from reality. If your mind is constantly in a dark place, if the black dog (a term coined by Winston Churchill when discussing his own battles with depression) is following you, hurting yourself takes your mind from a place of despair and channels all that attention elsewhere. Self-harm is redirection, taking an internal pain and briefly ignoring it by causing an external pain.

The popular misconception here is 'Oh you're only doing that for attention.' This is, for lack of a better term, a bullshit argument. Even if that were true, do you not think a person who is putting themselves in physical danger deserves some attention instead of sarcastic remarks? That aside, most self-harmers keep their pain secret, most live with it as a burden, anyone that knows this sort of pain knows what kind of toll it can take on your head box, and we who have experienced this, can help. If you have self-harmed, ask for help. See a doctor: they will not look at you with shame, they will not judge you, what you have done is dealt with a situation in the way your bananas brain told you would help – now let someone else help you deal with it.

Like with all mental health problems, it is not a weakness. No problem that is wired into your foggy noggin is a weakness; we are all dealing with our internal struggles in our own ways, as sufferers we have all hit bottom, we have all seen a darkness we didn't think we'd be able to escape, our responsibility as a community is to talk, listen, to start a conversation about these stigmas (a subject I will cover in greater detail further on) and help each other. An important takeaway from mental health conversations, and if you only take one thing away from this book it should be this, is that you are not alone. Even if you feel completely isolated in your suffering, if you feel like no one will ever be able to contemplate the myriad of nonsense going on upstairs, you are not alone. There are charities to talk to* that are there to help; local NHS practices

---

* CALM, MIND, Samaritans, Anxiety UK are all wonderful and you can find contact details for them at the back of this book.

are now offering remote therapies, where you can discuss issues with doctors or trained mental health professionals through your computer; and there are forums and message boards where people will talk things through with you. Somewhere among the six billion people aimlessly wandering this planet, there will be someone who can relate to your situation and they will want to talk about it just as much as you do.

Suicide rates in the western world are rising, and it is one of the biggest killers of all genders. A suicide will directly affect six people, be those family members, partners or friends. To put it frankly, suicide is devastating. Suicide is a serious risk for anxiety sufferers because, as we have discussed, anxiety can infect every area of your life. These days, most of us will know someone or be someone who has lost someone to suicide. Some of us are suicide survivors. However devastating you know suicide to be, however horrific you know it is, the stigma is still there, the ideas of cowardliness and weakness are still annoyingly fucking prevalent in society and the media. Suicide is also an incredibly difficult thing to talk about: the connotations of it, the impact of it, the closeness some of us feel to it. It is difficult to discuss, especially in a book that is supposed to be half-funny-half-serious, but hey, fuck it, let's give it a go.

Here's my story. I was in my early twenties, I had been quite effective at self-destructing for a while, I didn't know where my life was going, I had very few friends, I felt alone. All of which was, upon reflection, untrue. I was doing okay – not great – at my job, there were people who cared for me, and at the other end of a phone there were people I could have spoken to at any point. But this is not how my brain worked then. I felt alone. Cripplingly alone. I stood in my bathroom staring at myself in the mirror, a bottle of cheap whisky sat on the counter and a razor blade on the edge of the sink. I had come to the conclusion that it was the right time to do it. I was even stupid enough to romanticise it, I pictured myself as one of my heroes, Nick Drake or Jeff Buckley. I convinced myself, and it was so clichéd, that it was better to burn out than fade away. And I had burned out. I sit now, writing this, reflecting on it properly for the first time since I did it, and just wondering, why? Hindsight is beautiful like that, but in the moment there is no hindsight, there is only the all-encompassing idea of finality.

Spoiler alert, I didn't die. I KNOW, what a twist. Just call me the new M. Night Shyamalan. I had gone to a place so dark I never thought I could get out of it. I found myself at a point I never thought I would experience, and I felt relieved. The thing with discussing suicide in this detail is that there is no answer to this, there is no comfort to be given to those who have suffered with this sort of loss, there are no absolute and definitive textbook answers that can be given to help people in the future; the internal bedlam that befalls sufferers is their own unique turmoil. While we wish we could hold people, shake it out of them, the human brain just doesn't work like that.

The one thing we can do as a society, not as a group of individuals but as a collective, is to provide support. This will make sure the funding is there for mental health support in the NHS and the private sector. Which will ensure that the stigma of this killer can be lifted, and that we can get ourselves into a position as a global community where we can look at these problems and let people know that they are not alone, even when, as I know all too well, you can feel like the loneliest, most lost person in the universe. The stigma can often be the killer.

If only people knew that help is out there, just on the other side of this black fog. This alienation can be unspeakably damaging, so it is our duty as human beings to help each other. No blame, no hurt, no responsibility should be felt by a single person. That is not what this is about and if you have been affected, please know that you should never feel that way. I mean, we can now order socks to our houses from our phone, so the least we can do is talk to one another.

Sorry we had to get all serious there for a moment, let's get ourselves a cup of tea or a cake or seventeen cakes and go back to the abstract weirdness you have hopefully started to enjoy.

7.
MY BRAIN VS. SOCIALISING

(AKA Facebook, Discount Shots and Birthday Ninjas)

Sartre said, 'Hell is other people.' I have always thought this quote was far too simplistic. Like maybe something got lost in translation. What I think Sartre meant was: 'Hell is meeting people for the first time, or meeting people you aren't used to, or spending any sort of time with people who don't fit into a select group of people you have deemed (after many years and a long process of examination) safe to be around.' I do apologise for starting a chapter with 'Sartre said' as that's how a majority of terrible philosophy essays start, but this is my book and that quote desperately needed fixing.

The world would be a beautiful place if it wasn't full of people. People are terrifying, people are mean, people are difficult. When you list the pros and cons next to each other, the lists differ in length substantially.

Cons: Humans are mean to other humans, humans are mean to animals, humans are mean to everything, humans spit on public transport, humans swear at you from their cars, humans are rude to waiters, humans litter, humans tell other humans to kill themselves on the Internet, humans watch *Mrs Brown's Boys*, humans voted for Donald Trump. Pros: Humans invented chips. Also there may be other pros but I am just sticking with the chips thing right now. Oh and maybe roast potatoes, and Birds Eye potato waffles. Actually, just any potato-based snacklet. As anyone who has ever worked in hospitality can tell you, hell is other people. Dammit, that quote DOES work.

Social anxiety is one of the most common ways in which generalised anxiety presents itself. Remember when you were a kid and your parents had their friends round and they would make you come downstairs and talk to them and be sociable? It's like that, multiplied by a thousand. In day-to-day life, we surround ourselves with people we trust. We all have our own vetting processes in order to decide whether a human being is worthy of our time or not. You don't instantly become friends with every single person you interact with. That would be ridiculous. We all can't be Tom on Myspace. We carefully choose our friends, our lovers, our partners, and if you aren't up to a set of standards we have invented then you don't make the cut. The problem is that there are people everywhere. Have you been outside lately? They are absolutely bloody all over the place. It's horrifying. I haven't actively chosen to spend time with any of these people. I certainly haven't vetted the gentleman on this rush hour train who owns the armpit my face is currently stuck in.

It all comes down to trust: you feel safe around those you can trust, you can be yourself with these people or, at the very least, you feel comfortable enough to let your guard down a little bit. Anyone who makes you feel like you can be a little bit more like yourself is a good person in your life.

Your circle of friends will diminish as you get older. When you're in school you'll have a group of friends you would die for, because you're young and your brain hasn't realised that most human beings are a threat to your livelihood; there is still a fraction of hope there. When you hit university age, you have a small group of close friends – your gang – but you are beginning to grow suspicious that you may only be friends with these people through convenience. In your twenties you'll have enough friends to just about play a game of tennis doubles. In your thirties you'll have one or two close friends. In your forties you'll probably have kept one of your friends because, like a crap version of a TV reality show, you have whittled down the competition to one.

It's another way of defending ourselves. When you burn yourself on the kettle, you actively avoid doing that again because it was annoying, so we usually do the same with people: if we get burned once, we actively avoid that scenario from then on. We cut out any negative influences on our life and leave only those who support and care for us. Or at least we should, if people were sensible, but most of us are not. This doesn't just apply to those who suffer from anxiety, this is a general human rule. The idea that we try to pre-approve our social circles goes hand in hand with social anxiety. The fear of the unknown, the terror of disappointing someone, it's all there with new friendships. With close friends you have a comfort blanket, but with strangers, or figures of authority, that comfort blanket is set on fire and replaced with a blanket of spiders and night terrors. Too much? Too much.

'Why are we here?'
'To be sociable.'
'OK, but why?'
'We said we would . . .'
'1) We could go home and no one would notice if we were here or not. And 2) there are blankets and crisps at home, this place is completely devoid of blankets.'
'Yeah but there are crisps.'
'You know what I mean!'
'We don't do this very often, we can manage an hour.'
'AN HOUR? DO YOU KNOW WHAT COULD HAPPEN IN AN HOUR? The average small-talk conversation lasts two minutes, that's thirty conversations. You think you're up for handling THIRTY conversations?'
'Oh fuck no.'
'And what if someone asks about you in detail? You hate talking about yourself.'

'I hadn't thought of that.'
'This was a terrible idea.'
'This was a terrible idea.'

So what do you do? You have to be sociable. It's part of living as a human being. We are a sociable species. We didn't invent three shots for £5 to do them by ourselves. Most of the time the solution is the same one we apply to any problem your mind throws at you: you fake it. And you fake it hard. Most people with any form of anxiety are proficient in faking it in some way or another. Mostly because if we all walked around vocalising our inner torments then we'd be thrown into a padded cell. When asked how you are, it's more socially acceptable to reply 'Fine thank you' than 'Well I don't want to be here, I am tired, this place is too busy, I am out of my comfort zone, also you seem nice and therefore you intimidate me, also I saw a dog on the way here and that was the highlight of the evening and I will write about that in my mood journal when I get home. You?' If you start conversations like that, people usually just give you a half-hearted smile and edge away very slowly. So you lie. We all lie. The greatest lie in the world is thinking that anyone knows what they are doing with their lives. We are all faking it. We are all terrified. We are all hoping that we can get through today without incident, and then hoping the same thing the next day, and every day after that until a piano falls on us.

We are all faking it. It's just that some of us are

better at it than others, that's all. The moment you realise that no fucking person on this planet has any idea what they are doing, you can calm down a bit. You are not abnormal for feeling lost, you are not a freak for being uncertain – we all are. It's human nature. We all aspire to be and do things that are out of our reach, but we are doing our damn best and putting on a good front. I can only speak from personal experience but my social anxiety derives from fear. I am so terrified that I am going to be a disappointment to the people I am with, or not interesting enough, or not funny enough, that I force myself into this swirl of panic that I can't get out of. And guess what? Being a ball of worry, and panic, and self-doubt, makes you a really dull person to be around! Oh, cruel irony!

As much as I can figure, there are four different types of socialising: socialising with colleagues; hanging out with friends; being around your family; and finally, meeting strangers.

Dilemma 1: Socialising with colleagues

Workplace relationships are relationships of circumstance. If you get on with your colleagues, you have hit gold. If not, bury your head in your work and who gives a fuck? You can be that weirdo in the office. That can be your gimmick. Embrace your weirdness. Fill the toaster with frogs (please don't do this). There are no laws saying you need to hang around with the people you work with. There are a few unavoidable exceptions though. Birthdays, where you gather around a cake in the break room and sing happy birthday to what's-her-face with the bad eyebrows in Accounts. That's easy because you can slip into the crowd and no one will notice you. You are the birthday ninja. Work-based relationship-building events (the career equivalent of being put into teams at school) usually involve some mundane task that enrages every member of the company and culminates in everyone agreeing that the business should have just spent the money on a massive piss-up in the pub next to the office. Team-building/office-based fun can be dealt with: there will be tasks to complete, objectives to be met, ways to distract your brain as you endure this forced socialisation.

Then comes the big daddy: the work Christmas party. There is an unwritten rule of British life: if you have not embarrassed yourself at a Christmas party once you simply haven't lived. It's a rite of passage. It is inescapable. Unlike team-building days, there is only one objective here and that is to drink. As someone who has had a panic attack at their last two Christmas parties I can offer advice. Steer the conversations away from yourself, ask questions. If you are unfamiliar with the person you are speaking to, ask questions, keep them talking – if they are talking, you can be the awesome listener. Find people you like, or at least don't actively avoid, and cling to them like a child holding their mother's leg on the first day of school, only with less urine seeping through your trouser leg. Lastly, don't stay if you are uncomfortable, it will be a recurring theme in this book but if you are not happy with the situation you are in, you are allowed to remove yourself from it. You have tried, you turned up, and next time you'll manage ten minutes longer. And then the next time you'll last ten minutes longer than that. Overcoming these problems is a slow process, and the only person rushing you is you.

Dilemma 2: Hanging out with friends

This is the easiest scenario to deal with, but not without its own difficulties (isn't anxiety fun?!) As I said earlier, your friends should be some of the only people who you are happy letting your guard down around. But let's not go over the top here, we are still talking about a social situation and it still holds its problems. My best friend also suffers from social anxiety and we meet once a week in an old pub in Hackney and catch up on life. Can you guess how a conversation starts between two grown men with social anxiety? That's right: awkwardly. We have known each other for seventeen years, yet we still both fear making a tit of ourselves, or putting a word out of place, or offending the other one. A pint in and we are fine, the alcohol has allowed our brains to spill out of our mouths. I think this shows that anxiety isn't exclusive, it's not limited to certain scenarios, it just makes you wary of every single scenario. What I have learned from these interactions is that I am not alone, and this is one of the lessons about any sort of mental health that doesn't get screamed out loud enough, so let's do that now: YOU ARE NOT ALONE.

When your mind is always on the lookout for threats it's extremely difficult to relax and this is one quality that friendship can provide: relaxation. At the back of your mind you will still be thoroughly aware of everything that could go wrong at any moment, but with true friends, if you do make a complete dick of yourself they won't care. They know you, they know your conditions and your fears, and they will help. With anxiety, your friends are your support group. They are the people you can text at midnight with your woes and they will often reply (unless they are early sleepers in which case, who the hell goes to bed at midnight?!). They will distract you, they will send you funny things they have found on the Internet, they will help. I think this is why a majority of those with anxiety problems turn to social media. The distraction of constant updates, a myriad of things to preoccupy your brain at your fingertips, it can almost be seen as therapy. We will get into social media in more depth in a later chapter, but for now let's do some tips on how to be friends with crazy people!

Honesty is the best policy, again

If you have been friends with someone for a very long time, there is a high chance you have seen each other at your best and at your worst. They stood by you as you achieved your goals, as you celebrated birthdays, but they probably also stood by you when you got dumped or threw up off that bridge that time. Mates will see us at our greatest and our least graceful, that's what friendship is, so listen, talk, be a shoulder to have an existential crisis on. Be the friend that you would want if you were going through that situation.

Keep tabs on your friend's mental health

If you spend enough time around another human being you start to pick up on their little quirks. The way they scrunch up their face when they are annoyed, or the way they turn up on your doorstep at 3 a.m. covered in cat blood – there are little ways to notice if something is wrong. You will know when someone isn't themselves, it can the tiniest of mannerisms but you will instantly know. It's also OK to ask them periodically if they are OK. Just a quick and honest message to see how they are coping with the world at the moment. Send them funny articles and images; if you can keep reminding them that someone out there is thinking about them, even if it doesn't feel like it's working, having the knowledge that another human being simply gives a shit can be an amazing thing.

Be there when you can

One of the greatest things to help anxiety (along with other mental health disorders) is a little distraction. You don't have to do much, your presence will usually be all they need. Try to make them go out with you, to go to the cinema or for a walk, just something to get out of themselves for a little bit. If they can't handle the outside world, just sit with them at home and let them know that you are there if they need you. Provide blankets, snacks and put on a bad movie, trust me when I say the other person will simply appreciate the company. You don't have to go above and beyond the call of duty if you don't want to, just help in a way that you would want to be helped.

Dilemma 3: Family

This obviously depends entirely on your family relationship and whether you are in contact with your family, etc. But for argument's sake let's say you have a decent relationship with the people that you are genetically blackmailed to spend time with. If there is one thing I have learned from battling a myriad of mental health problems it's that honesty is the best policy. This works twofold. First, your parents will hopefully respect you for telling them. Your parents love you and want you to be okay – that's what parents do, and if you are struggling, your parents will want to help, or at least make you a nice cup of tea and talk about old memories to distract you. Second, it's a handy way to find out if it is a genetic family trait. There are many schools of thought on whether mental illnesses can be traced through genetics and your doctor will ask this, your therapist will ask this, so it can be a helpful thing to know.

There are many generational differences when it comes to mental health problems. These largely come down to the stigma and ignorance surrounding them. Thankfully though, now that mental health is being talked about in the media, and in a more accepting light, it has become a little easier to discuss than it was previously. On the other side, it was only a hundred years ago that soldiers with PTSD were shot for 'being deserters' rather than seen as innocent men suffering with crippling mental health problems. It was only fifty years ago that people were still receiving electroshock therapy for depression or post-natal depression. When you quantify progress in these terms, it's amazing how far we have come.

But it can also demonstrate why those of an older generation, or an old-school way of thinking, can find mental health a difficult subject to get their heads around. This is all about education. If you fear that your family will ever say 'You just need to calm down' or 'Oh, all you young people have something wrong with you', you can make one of two choices. Either take it upon yourself to educate them, or never mention it to them again. I do encourage the first one: it's better for you, it's better for them and it's better for your relationship. If you are battling a chemical imbalance in your brain, you have about as much control over it as you do over the place you were born. As generations become more open about mental health, we can learn together and be more accepting. With such a large percentage of the population experiencing some form of mental health problem in their lives (roughly 25%)*

---

* https://www.mind.org.uk/information-support/types-of-mental-health-problems/statistics-and-facts-about-mental-health/how-

it is more than likely that your parents have been through something, or at the very least can identify with how you are feeling right now.

Dilemma 4: Meeting strangers

First impressions are important and, to those with an anxious disposition, an extremely difficult activity to partake in. I am still haunted by receiving my coffee from a barista and replying to 'I'm sorry we don't have any cardboard sleeves left' with: 'You too!' Interacting with people you don't know is an unavoidable event in life. It could include having a haircut end up in an elaborate lie because the hairdresser asks where you are going on holiday but you can't afford a holiday so you create a version of you that is going to St Lucia for the summer. Or the unavoidable tasks of going to the supermarket, work meetings, weddings or birthday parties, even meeting distant relatives for the first time – these are all accompanied by a sense of fear and foreboding and an irrational worry that clouds the entire conversation. What fuels this dread is an underlying layer of uncertainty. Will your palms be too sweaty for a handshake? Will your handshake be too strong or too weak? Do you even do a handshake? Is this an awkward hug moment? Oh God you went in for the handshake and it turned into a hug and you accidentally touched their breast. Why are you like this?

I repeat, the way to get through this is to fake it. Your

common-are-mental-health-problems/

mind will be screaming at you to run, to get yourself out of this situation in any way possible, but the most you can ask of yourself in this scenario is to do your best and don't put yourself in a position you don't want to be in. I know that in this chapter I have expressed my disdain for the human race in several blunt ways but, to be brutally honest – and it does pain me to say so – humans can be very understanding. No one expects more of you than yourself. This is a sentiment that can be easily forgotten, or simply ignored in favour of blaming yourself. It is so much easier to be hard on yourself than it is to be kind to yourself. Public interactions are out of your comfort zone; if you know this, you can handle this. It's terribly clichéd to say that admitting something is the first step, but once you can recognise your triggers you can start to control them. It can be something as small as 'Last time I went out I only managed half an hour, this time I am going to do forty minutes.' Once again, you are your worst critic and you doubt yourself more than anyone else ever would.

So, breathe. Know your exits so that you feel safe. Identify the people you are most comfortable around. Drink water instead of alcohol. These are just some suggestions, but you will know what makes you feel most comfortable here. I need to say something about the hug/handshake/air-kiss situation because I get serious anxiety about this from the moment I start a meeting, because I know I'll have to pick one at the end. The best technique that I've found is to just take the lead – pick one and stick to it.

If there was one takeaway message for this chapter, it would be this. The self-imposed criteria by which we judge ourselves are entirely fictional. In a 'normal' human mind they are the brain's way of pushing us towards our aspirations, a set of goals to ensure we don't assimilate into our sofas, to challenge and test us, or at the very least to keep us active and give us drive. But in the maddening frenzy of an anxious cerebrum, these are heightened. Mostly because anxiety is a dick. One of the most peculiar things about social anxiety is how it can manifest itself out of nothingness. For some it can be a lifetime constant, an underlying terror surrounding any interaction we have ever encountered. For others it suddenly appears one day, like a stray cat scratching at the front door. Before you know it the bastard is in the house, eating your food, ruining your sofas, pissing on everything, and has decided, much against your wishes, to stay.

And how has this all affected me? At one point in my life I was a very outgoing person, I tolerated people, to a degree, and I could hold conversations with a faint touch of normality. I placed myself as a self-deprecating joker, which upon reflection was probably a guise for an already prevalent self-esteem issue. But in general, I was sociable. Then one day I was terrified to leave the house and completely and irrationally afraid of interacting with another human being. In this situation every possible paranoid question spills out of your anxious brain and fills your head as you try to answer them all at once, but eventually you succumb to the insecurities and convince yourself that you are worthless, uninteresting, embarrassing, boring, annoying and basically just an awful human being unworthy of the attention of others. It can feel impossible to get yourself out of this place, but like a documentary about a really small pop band, it's all about tiny Steps. (Oh, that was painful.)

TIPS FOR HANDLING SOCIAL ANXIETY:

⚡ Identify your comfort zones

We are most comfortable when we feel safe. That safety can be a place or a person. If you are feeling anxious about going somewhere, pick a place you know – perhaps a place you've been to many times – and you will feel like you are battling on home ground. If your safety blanket is a person (a partner, a friend, a colleague) ask them to join you, to support you, then if worst comes to worst, you have someone you know to speak to and to make light of the situation you are in.

⚡ The only person demanding more from you is you

This may be a recurring theme in this book, but stop being so fucking hard on yourself. The people you meet aren't expecting you to be the best person in the entire world, they are expecting you to be you. My social anxiety derives from crippling low self-esteem – a need to impress and show off and create a persona that people will like. Your friends, your colleagues, your family, know that this isn't you. They aren't expecting anything of you, just your company, which is important to them, so take a deep breath and do what you can.

⚡ Excuse yourself when you need to

Yes, it's that pesky flight response again, but sometimes you need it. If you start to feel like you can't handle this, or that you are uneasy, feeling ill or like your brain is on fire, bail. You are allowed to. Go home, make a cup of tea and think about what caused you to leave. The crowd? The noise? The fear that you were boring? Identify that and rationalise it and use it to help you in the next scenario. Because in the end – in the nicest possible way – no one else cares as much as you. Trust me.

⚡ Look after yourself, you dick!

No one can look after you like you. Real life is not like in the films where you are saved by the strapping hero – you have to save yourself. Yes, other people can help you stand back up, but you're the one who has to remain standing. (Yes, that's fucking cheesy but I am having a moment here leave me alone.) Don't put yourself in situations you know you can't handle. Breathe. Self-care is vital here.

⚡ Practice makes perfect

I am not the biggest fan of immersion therapy, but I am managing my social anxiety one step at a time.

Months ago I couldn't sit in a pub with people I've known for years without feeling like I needed to run, but now I can sit with people I don't really know. It's still difficult, but it's an improvement. It's baby steps. Try half an hour of being sociable, then next time try forty-five minutes. Don't put too much pressure on yourself, but push yourself that extra little bit and you'll be able to fall into a pattern you can handle. It's like stretching: right now I can't touch my toes but with daily stretching, I'd have my leg over my shoulder in no time. Probably. I'm not going to try this.

To make it seem real, you have to look at the pros and cons of being sociable. Pro: you get to go out and see your friends. Con: awkwardness. Pro: you get to leave your house. Con: you have to leave your house. Pro: in the outside world there is alcohol and dogs and cool things to Instagram and maybe someone dropped a tenner on the ground. Con: maybe that tenner you found on the ground is laced with LSD and now you're drugged you'll get sold to a Mexican drug cartel and made to dance at fancy parties for rich bearded men. I'm getting off track. In the end, going out is healthy, staying in all the time isn't healthy and you're working to become healthy, so get out there. Get out there and give them hell.

8.
MY BRAIN VS. RELATIONSHIPS

(AKA Gammon, Smut and Antique Swimming Goggles)

'Do you think they even know I'm alive?'

'Probably not.'

'Good lord they are so beautiful . . .'

'Yeah and we look like the Elephant Man and a whoopee cushion had a baby.'

'I'm going to go talk to them.'

'And say what? "Hi, I'm socially awkward", then throw up on them?'

'I'm going to die alone aren't I?'

'Of course not, you have me!'

So you've met someone. They are attractive, they are funny, they are intelligent, they like all the things you like, they even share your theories on the existence of Bigfoot, they laugh at your jokes, they genuinely seem to not hate being in your presence. It's got to be a trick? Right? The anxious voice at the back of your head just keeps telling you that this is all an elaborate practical joke, that at any moment a TV presenter is going to pop out from underneath the table and scream 'YOU HAVE BEEN PRANKED'. Self-doubt, low self-esteem, lack of confidence, constantly expecting the worst to happen . . . anxiety keeps all these thoughts circling in your mind as the person who has agreed to spend time with you talks about their job or their collection of antique swimming goggles or something . . . oh God you haven't been listening, you've spent the last five minutes wondering if you have something in your teeth, or if maybe one of your eyebrows fell off without your knowledge and now you're just panicking, oh God they're still talking! Just say 'Indeed', and take a sip of wine. Thank God, it doesn't look like they noticed.

Anxiety thrives on loneliness. When your anxiety tells you that everything is a threat – going outside, speaking to other people, socialising, everything basically – it's an easy solution to retreat into yourself. You can avoid it all by staying at home, back in your blanket fort, covered in crisps and writing melancholy poetry that only you will read because frankly it's bloody awful and how many times do I have to tell you that 'clouds' doesn't rhyme with 'sadness'. While disappearing into yourself can be preferable, anxiety throws you another curveball: an absolute and utter fear of loneliness.

We've all met that person who says, 'I am really good when I'm on my own', and that's probably true, but there is a difference between being comfortable in your own company and becoming a hermit who drinks their own urine and starts throwing beans at passers-by for enjoying themselves while being bean-flinging distance from you. Learning to be comfortable in your own skin is an important weapon in your anxiety ass-kicking battle, especially if you are, like me, inclined to associate being alone with not being able to get out of bed for days or finding yourself in a pattern of complete self-destruction. With the beautiful thing that is social media, we are only ever 140 characters* away from interaction with another human being. You keep in your pocket your own social circle. So when you feel the shadow of loneliness looming over you, you can post something, anything, and people will reply, or you can simply lurk and see what conversations are happening in the world at that time.

DATING

Dating is horrible. No one enjoys dating. People enjoy all the gross stuff they do when they are naked with each other but the small talk over an overpriced bowl of pasta in a brightly lit restaurant with what basically equates to a stranger? No one enjoys that. The basic premise of dating is auditioning another human being

---

* When I wrote this it was 140 characters, and now of course twitter has increased their limit to 280 and RUINED this sentiment.

to see if you will grant them permission to touch your genitals. That's it. Not to be blunt, but let's be honest here. As humans we crave the love of other people. For people who spend most of their time actively trying to avoid other humans, their anxious mind struggles and fights for a relationship where the other person will hug you and tell you that you are not losing your mind. We crave comfort, we crave acceptance, and to get this you have to date people. You don't want to just pick the first person you find, you have to test them, evaluate them, quiz them, are they good enough for you? Are they *good* for you?

My own dating history has been, let's say, a confusing journey into terrifying nonsense, so I won't sit here and tell you the correct way to date another person. That would be hypocritical, and more than likely excruciating for both of us. I do however have some mediocre advice. Do things at your own pace. With the sense of order and regime built into the mind of an anxiety-ridden wreck, it can be so easy to fall into a circle of comparative competition. You see your friends on Facebook hitting thirty with their kids, their pets, their three-bedroom house in the country, and you see yourself alone, in a one-bed flat in a less than desirable part of north London. The whole 'I'm hitting this birthday next year and I haven't even done this yet' line is outdated and dangerous. It may have made sense when life expectancy was forty and we needed to procreate at an irrational rate to adhere to some form of social normality, but now that life expectancy is rising and every public resource is at breaking point there is NO RUSH. It is only more pressure you are putting on yourself.

You don't need 'a life plan', you need to look after yourself. Nothing in this world is more important than your own mental and physical well-being. Put everything else second. When you are comfortable enough to dip your toe into the world of dating, go for it, but only when you want to. Other things to note, never let anyone make you feel like shit. If they do, catapult that person out of your life immediately. Don't change yourself to impress anyone, Sandy in *Grease* can fucking do one in my opinion. You are you, and you are fucking awesome. And if you're in a relationship, don't let it engulf your entire personality. You are two individuals in a couple, not only a couple.

When hurling yourself into the dating world there is one thing to remember: you are your own worst critic. Every morning I stare at my own disaster of a face in the mirror, I think to myself 'You look like someone covered a mannequin in gammon and chucked it through an orchard of barber shop hair and regret.' When your brain is wired to low self-esteem and non-existent body confidence, thinking that anyone would ever want to be near you, let alone touch you, can be bizarre to comprehend. But the idea you have of yourself is completely different from how other people see you. You can think that you look like a sack of porridge in ill-fitting garments, with the personality of a concussed starfish and the charm of a bin on fire, but to someone else, you can be everything. People are weird like that.

I mean, if Charles Manson can get laid while he's in prison, you can definitely get laid. (Don't go and bang Charles Manson, that's not where I am going with this.) Another hurdle to awkwardly skip over in the track event of anxiety is self-esteem. Personally I think the twenty-first-century poet and philosopher Ru Paul says it best, 'If you can't love yourself, how in the hell you gonna love somebody else?'

Once again we are arguing with our irrational brain. We know we don't look half as bad as we convince ourselves that we do, we know what we perceive as flaws in ourselves won't be seen like that by anyone else, but Mr Irrational Brain keeps screaming negativity at you, while Rational Brain, who actually thinks you quite look cute today, can't be heard over the din of negativity. It's not egotistical to believe in yourself, it's not vain to think you look nice today, it's not conceited to think you've got this. You *do* have this. You are the only you out there and anyone would be lucky to even be near you.

In researching this book I delved into the world of self-help books with titles such as 'LOVE URSELF', 'YOU ARE VALID' and 'SELF LOVE' in an attempt to see if my confidence (or lack thereof) could be improved upon. If you have never read a self-help book, most are written by good-looking Americans who run seminars that involve them wearing large headset microphones and screaming into a theatre of people who have paid £1,000 to learn how to be better at life (my first tip would be: don't waste £1,000 on seminars). All of the authors are called things like 'Groban' or 'Dr Fantastic' or some such nonsense, and their way of improving your life is through the art of shouting at you.

'YOU FEELING GOOD TODAY? YOU SHOULD BE FEELING GOOD. BECAUSE TODAY IS A GOOD DAY. YEAH! YOU ARE GOOD TODAY. WHAT DO YOU WANT OUT OF LIFE? THAT'S RIGHT. LIFE ITSELF. NOW LISTEN TO THIS SAXOPHONE SOLO I PLAY WITH MY ARSE!'

OK, the last bit might be a bit of an exaggeration. Here is my attempt at running a self-help seminar:

'Morning. Now, are you a dickhead? OK, to stop being a dickhead have you maybe tried not being a dickhead? One thousand pounds please.'

It's a simple golden rule of life: don't be a dickhead, don't think of yourself as a dickhead, don't let anyone treat you like a dickhead. Learning to love yourself takes more than repeating 'I am valid' in the mirror three times every morning, especially if you get it wrong and say 'Vlad' in the mirror three times instead and Vlad the Impaler turns up and ruins your day.

TIPS ON GETTING A LITTLE BIT OF SELF-CONFIDENCE BACK:

⚡ **Give yourself a fucking break.** Yeah I know I say that a lot, but you are the one who is putting the most pressure on yourself. Look in the mirror. Breathe in all the negative thoughts your irrational brain is throwing at you: 'I wish my nose was a bit different.' Now listen to your rational brain for a minute. 'Actually my nose is unique, it's my nose, it's cute as fuck.'

⚡ **Treat Yo' Self.** Get your hair done. Get yourself a new dress or a new jacket, get something you can wear and even your irrational brain goes 'Fuuuuck' and then wolf-whistles at you.

⚡ **Only contribute to conversations when you want to.** If you're feeling anxious and feel like you're not talking enough, don't worry. If you're anxious and won't stop talking, take a deep breath, count to four, release for four and see if that has helped with the nonsensical word purge that's happening in your gob. Talking too much can be a symptom of anxiety and often your own anecdotes can get away from you as your brain goes at 100x its usual rate, panicking so much you've accidentally put yourself on fast forward. Ask questions, laugh at your own jokes, believe in every word that falls out of your gob.

⚡ **Don't do anything you don't want to do.** Don't like Mexican food? Don't go to a Mexican restaurant. Don't like someone you've met? Leave the date. (Leave the date in a nice way though; fake a heart attack or accidentally start a fire.) Don't let anyone tell you how to dress or what to do. You are awesome and you are fighting anxiety, so you're basically a superhero, albeit a bit of a crap superhero but a superhero all the same.

My own relationships have been marred by my mental health problems, leading to break-ups, self-sabotage and poor life choices. When the tiny man that is anxiety is constantly whispering in your ear that you are not good enough for this person or not good enough for that person, you start to believe them. I decided to speak to Mia Vaughan, who I follow on Twitter but who also has a popular blog called Cigarettes and Calpol in which she discusses her life with anxiety and her daughter (follow it, it's rather fantastic). I asked her how her anxiety affected her relationships.

'Relationships are actually one of the main things my anxiety likes to mess with. I have a horrible tendency to assume the worst and convince myself it is absolute gospel. If a friend posts a subtweet I convince myself it *must* be about me, if my boyfriend doesn't text back he's 100% sleeping with someone else (and she has better hair), if absolutely nothing happens and I'm sat quite happily watching telly I somehow manage to decide that all my friends hate me and are currently having a secret meeting discussing it. It's pretty exhausting.'

The anxious brain doesn't just jump to conclusions, it pole-vaults over them into a new territory of ridiculousness. Your worst fears are projected into your senses, and when it comes to relationships, betrayal is a common paranoid symptom. Anxiety can leave you helpless, a victim of your own overactive imagination. It's not like you can use immersion therapy to solve this particular problem with anxiety. Seeing a room full of people throwing shade about you probably won't help you get over your fear of your friends hating you. The thing with friends though, is that you can just ask:

'Was that subtweet about me?'
'No, for the eight hundredth time, no, are you aware that not everything is about you?'
'I find that hard to believe.'
'I love you, but you're an idiot'

Let's talk about sex, baby, let's talk about . . . wait no that would be terribly inappropriate. I don't have much advice to give on this subject; my own inadequacies aside, there are a few things that shouldn't even need to be said.

⚡ Your sex life is your sex life. As long as it's between consenting adults then no one else should give a flying fuck.

⚡ Your body is your body, do with it whatever the fuck you want to. Get whatever you want pierced, shove whatever you want up wherever you want. That's your choice. Just be safe and clean piercings regularly.

⚡ Never judge another human being for *their* choices in *their* sex life.

⚡ Don't put yourself in any position (figuratively and literally) that you are not comfortable with.

Now that's cleared up, sex and anxiety don't particularly get on well with each other. Sex is you at your most vulnerable, with all your wobbly bits out and another human being looking at you and oh God don't look at me, actually let's turn off the lights, actually I'll go into the other room and leave you to it. Actually, an erotic novel where one of the characters has severe anxiety would probably help with representation . . .

The Sexy Worrier By Rusty Cricket
(I've decided that's my smut writer name)

Chapter 4 – A sexy sex time

He stood there, his naked body jiggling about like a ham in a hurricane. She lay on the bed, inviting him over. His left foot was cold because he got too excited and only had time to take one sock off. As he approached the bed he remembered that he had left the living window open a little bit and now was wondering if robbers would enter the house mid-coitus. 'What are you thinking?' she asked, seductively. 'Oh, about you,' he lied, convinced murderers were getting ready to burst into the front room. His foot was still cold.

'Are you OK?' he asked even though he hadn't really done anything yet.

'Yes?' she asked, perplexed.

'Do you need a drink of water?' he enquired.

'No, can we just . . .' she said, like a sexy . . . thing.

'Yes, sorry,' he moaned.

'Stop saying sorry,' she said, seductively, again.

'Sorry,' he replied.

'You're on my hair!' she squealed.

'Sorry,' he retorted, in a very sexy way, 'Are you OK?'

She stared directly into his eyes. 'Stop fucking asking me if I am OK.'

'Sorry.'

'Stop saying sorry!'

Neither of them finished. They decided to play a game of Scrabble instead. She won with a triple word score for 'Disappointed'.

Of course that's an over-exaggeration. As I said before, the way you see yourself, and all the negativity, lives in *your* head, no one else's. Never underestimate yourself. Right, that's enough about sex. Basically you'll be fine, just don't do anything you don't want to, got it? Good. Right now we all have to go and pray and get all this sin off of us before moving on.

You've found someone you think you really like. You've found someone who makes you feel more like you when you're near them. You've found someone you can trust. What next?

RUN. PANIC. FLEE. No, don't do that, you dick. Don't fall into patterns of self-destruction, don't avoid something good happening to you because Mr or Miss Irrational Brain is whispering paranoia into your lust-filled noggin. Tiny anxiety battle #302: trusting people.*

Imagine a safe. A high-tech safe with fingerprint analysis and eye recognition. Before you get to the safe there are sixteen doors all with different codes, and laser tripwires, and guard dogs, and a guard pigeon for some reason. The contents of the safe are your real emotions and the other human being has to get past all the other barriers before you can let them in to see the real you. It's just our brain protecting us from getting hurt, you're not an emotionally stunted person, you are just overly cautious. Letting someone see the real you is a big deal, a privilege that you will bestow upon very few people in your lifetime, and even then you will worry and agonise and worry some more about letting someone else in. The criteria by which you do this are yours and yours alone. Once you feel comfortable with someone, once you think, 'Oh fucking hell I might actually like this person', you can go from there. But this of course leads to one more thing: telling your partner you have anxiety.

It can feel like you're revealing a dark and terrible secret about yourself. Like telling your partner you have eleven toes and they are all on the one foot, or telling your partner you have seen Mumford & Sons live three times, there are some things you put off telling someone just in case they freak out and run away. Anxiety is a

---

* I have no idea if it is number 302 by the way, I just know I have written 'anxiety battle' loads of times by now.

part of you but it's not your entire personality. It's a small defect, like a birthmark that looks like the Pope or the eleven-toes-on-one-foot thing (OK maybe more like a birthmark). It will be with you for your entire life, so it's just about handling it, trusting this person to move into your selected support network and allowing someone to help you. I apologise for my use of personal anecdotes in this book, but this is the way I told my wife I had anxiety. Or, to be honest, this is the way my wife found out I have anxiety.

Before being diagnosed I knew I had pretty bad anxiety, I am pretty sure my now wife (we were dating at this time) had a slight inkling because of the following story. We were stood in Toulouse airport, getting ready to board an 8 a.m. plane to Gatwick. As I've mentioned, airports and I don't mix. I had got through the check-in, constantly worrying that our tickets would be wrong, I had got through security despite the terror that I must have accidentally packed a bomb – I had no idea how I would have done it, the entire notion is completely nonsensical, but as the gigantic French man patted me down I had convinced myself they would find something and I would end up in a French prison and be traded for baguettes. Of course that didn't happen, but my body was brimming with adrenaline at this point, my muscles were tense, I was sweating.

While we were wandering through the usual duty-free shops looking at the cheap perfume, cigarettes you can purchase by the wardrobe-full, fancy booze I could never afford, I kept an eye on the time, knowing that the gate closed at 7.40 a.m., so we needed to be there by 7 a.m. at the latest, in case it was one of those weird gates where you have to get a bus to the plane. I have to leave time for these things. It was 6.50. We kept wandering. 6.55. I announced that we were going to have to go to the gate, my breath was quickening, my hand clenching on the strap of my backpack on my shoulder. She told me that she just needed to look at one more shop, on the other side of the airport, in the direction away from our gate. Nope. Panic attack time. My schedule had been thrown into disarray. Of course we had plenty of time, and the walk from one side of the airport to the other was about two minutes, but that's the rational part of the brain talking, the irrational part of my brain was at DEFCON 5. Or DEFCON 1. Whichever is the worst DEFCON. That alarm noise from *Kill Bill* was going off in my head: It was now 7.01 a.m. We were almost definitely going to miss our plane (even though the gate didn't close for another thirty-nine minutes), I would have to pay for another flight, the day was ruined, the week was ruined, I couldn't afford another flight, we lived in the airport now, no escape, oh God, I don't want to work at Sunglass Hut.

A full panic attack ensued, and at that point I had no idea what the bloody hell was happening. My wife asked if I was OK. 'Stop talking to me!' I snapped. One of the first times I snapped at her. We were both shocked. After three little bottles of Johnnie Walker Black, sat on our flight with loads of time to spare, I turned to her and simply said: 'I think I might have really bad anxiety.' Her response was, quite typically, comforting: 'You think?!'

The point of this story is that usually the other person will know well before you tell them. They may not have a full understanding of anxiety, not having it themselves and all, but they will know that something is different and they still like you regardless. You're still you, there's just a little bit more to you.

HOW TO TALK TO YOUR PARTNER ABOUT ANXIETY:

⚡**Start at the very beginning, a very good place to start.** 'I have anxiety' will often be met with 'Yeah I kind of figured' or 'OK, what would you like to do next?'

⚡**Talk about recovery and getting help with your partner.** Remember that it will affect them too. Tell them you want to go the doctor and talk it through with them. Tell them you might go and see a therapist. Tell them you might need to change a few aspects of your lifestyle. And tell them to hold your hand while you do all this.

⚡**Be honest.** Tell them everything. Tell them your triggers, what can set off a panic attack, your phobias; if you want to be completely honest, tell them that you're worried that they'll think you're weird for having anxiety (they probably think you're weird regardless of your anxiety, and that's why they like you).

You've added another person to your support network. It's like collecting Pogs but with emotional vulnerability and sad face emojis. You've told someone your deepest darkest secret, so now what do you have to do? Four words. LOCK. THAT. SHIT. DOWN. Trap them. Lay out a net so they can't go anywhere. Trick them with their stupid *feelings* and *emotions* towards you and make sure they never leave. It's the only sane thing to do.

Or you could just ask them to move in with you. That's probably more sensible. The dreaded cohabitation stage of a relationship. You can't afford to buy a house because you spent all your money on dating a person, so you do what every human has to do: rent the worst apartment you can find that is highly inconvenient for work and smells a bit like someone filled a fish with cabbage and exploded it all over the flat, but at least it's cheap! This is a rite of passage everyone must go through. You do not know yourself and you cannot test your relationship unless you have both lived in a rat-infested shoebox with a drunk landlord who lives below you who likes to learn the bagpipes at 3 a.m. It is the British way.

It's now anxiety's turn to try to trip you up again. You're happy? Well, fuck you here comes ANXIETY! If you find someone you can trust, who treats you well, who loves you, you get attached, it's a perfectly normal human reaction. Welcome back, our old friend, separation anxiety. As you identify another human being as a comfort blanket you associate them with one – as non-threatening – and your body floods itself with all the happy chemicals. In an anxious mind this can turn into a dependency, the relation of a feeling of safety with one single factor, a partner. This is referred to as creating an 'attachment figure'. When the partner is taken out of the equation – say they go to the shops to get you more biscuits for your pillow fort – your brain once again invents all kinds of impossible scenarios that may befall your attachment figure.

For instance, your partner has gone out with their friends and said they would be home at 10 p.m. It's 10.15. They haven't sent a message. You instantly assume they're dead. That's just where your brain goes to. Separation anxiety with attachment figures is just that, but all the time. It can manifest itself in many ways too, a refusal to go out unless you are accompanied by your attachment figure, nightmares where separation from your attachment figure is the main narrative, constantly imagining their death. It can even manifest itself as physical symptoms if separation is anticipated (headaches, feeling dizzy, feeling like you might barf like a spaniel). This form of separation anxiety is more common in children, and usually disappears at around toddler age, but it is becoming more and more prevalent in adults, especially those who have been hurt in past relationships or experienced very little stability in their upbringing. Within society this can be seen as just having a 'clingy' relationship. 'Oh you know Barry and Barrina?* They never do anything without each other! It's so weird!' This can be easily translated as: 'Oh you know Barry and Barrina? Well Barry has some separation anxiety issues that they are both working through at the moment, that's why they aren't out as much recently.' Like with most mental health disorders, rash personal judgements lack context, so never judge a book by its cover, never judge a song by its cover version. Dealing with this form of separation anxiety is about balance. You're allowed to want to spend all your time with your partner, you're allowed to dote on them and stab your initials into a tree for . . . why do people do that? Anyway, you're allowed to do these things, to be infatuated with each other, it's just not great if you have a panic attack every time they go to the shops to buy milk.

Of course all of this advice is purely circumstantial: you may identify as asexual, you may never want to get married, you may be comfortable being single, you might not be a people person. Your life, your rules. The purpose of these little snippets of nonsense is just to give you a few new weapons to put in your anxiety war chest. If you can take one piece of advice away from this chapter, or in fact this book in general, that affects your life in a positive way, we've done OK.

* Oh my God Barrina is an amazing name.

The Sexy Worrier By Rusty Cricket

Chapter 17 – A sexy role play

'You're a headmaster,' she whispered into his ear. 'And I'm a naughty schoolgirl.'

'Why are you naughty, what have you done?' he enquired.

'That doesn't matter,' she replied.

'Surely I need to know the severity of your actions to formulate a proper disciplinary procedure.'

'Jesus Christ, Barry . . .'

'Sorry, Barrina, this just doesn't make any sense—'

'OK I'm a naughty schoolgirl because . . .' She took a moment. A sexy moment. 'I was caught smoking behind the bike sheds.'

'Smoking will kill you, Barrina.'

'Can we have sex now?'

'Not until I find my other sock.'

9.

MY BRAIN VS. THE INTERNET

(AKA Selfies, Comments Sections and General Despair)

'Let's post a joke.'

'No. No one will laugh at it. No one will find it amusing. Everyone will judge you by it and you'll be internationally hated. People will send you death threats. People will burn down your house for your ill-handled attempts at "comedy".'

'But it's a half-decent joke about a dog—'

'Don't.'

'I did it.'

'Does it have a spelling mistake in it?'

'No . . .'

'Check again.'

'Oh God.'

'See. Now we have to join witness protection and move to a small town in middle America and become

friends with the guy who runs the gas station and then one night we will find out he is part of the Internet mafia.'

'I've deleted it.'

The first way you were able to e-express your complete and utter dejection for human existence with your friends and colleagues was by changing your MSN Messenger subheader to a Jeff Buckley lyric. Then we had Myspace, where you could drunkenly post 'bulletins' (for those of you too young to remember Myspace, it was basically just a massive angst rant that most people would ignore). These bulletins were mostly about how your life wasn't going the way you wanted it to, or how the girl you liked at school was dating someone in the same year as you who could actually grow a beard. Then you got angry that you couldn't grow a beard and tried to use MS Paint to crudely draw a beard on yourself. Then we got Facebook so we could, in real time, let our peers know our emotional state, and where in the world we were having an existential crisis. 'Aaron is losing the will to live – In a Tesco'. Then Twitter fell into our laps, so we could micro-blog our slowly crumbling mental state to the entire world.

Behind every social media status there is emotion. I'll admit that 90% of these emotions are either 'I am EXTREMELY ANGRY about . . .' or 'LOOK AT THIS FUCKING CAT', but between these less than subtle conversation starters are genuine chronicles of the human condition. Sometimes you need to look between the lines of a status to figure out how your friend or follower is doing mentally. Let's take me for example: I mostly write jokes, with some mental health blogs thrown in, with a dash of leftist political satire I'll admit . . . but mostly jokes. Bad jokes. Terrible jokes. This is because I find actual human interaction difficult, but I also like to make people laugh, and I do it behind a Twitter account because it's a barrier between me and any sort of situation in which I would feel uncomfortable. Basically, I use Twitter so much because I am utterly bananas.

There are two ways to look at the Internet. If you're a pessimist, you'll see the Internet as a rancid cesspool where the most unpleasant parts of humanity lurk only to throw insults at each other and find new horrific ways to sexualise everything in the world. Or, if you're a realist, you'll see it as a weird forum of idiots, everyone doing their own thing, and – like any spectrum of humanity – there are a few fuckwits. The analogy I use most often (and I apologise in advance for repeating it) is that the Internet is like a pub: it's playing good music, it's full of interesting people, it's just up to you where to sit and who with. Of course with anxiety, nothing can just be that easy. Every aspect of modern life must be evaluated and every interaction meticulously analysed for no reason. With the ability to access the entirety of human knowledge from a rectangle you keep in your pocket comes the knowledge that every movement you make online will be critiqued and criticised, and not only by your peers, but by random strangers from all around the globe, and most of them will hate you for no reason.

Saying that, the Internet is a haven for the mad among us. For something that has only been in existence in the general population for the last twenty years, and in the case of social media for the last twelve, it's become an inescapable necessity for many. The ability to link yourself to any other member of the human race from any other position on this hurtling space rock covered in monkeys is a new definition of community and a new way to find an escape. The point I am trying to make my way towards is that social media is a resource that previous generations didn't have, so when our parents and our parents' parents were simply told to 'get on with it' or 'cheer up' in regard to their mental health problems, we now have a generation who can converse, research and investigate their emotional well-being to an immense degree. For many, this can be the first time they realise they have an issue or a problem, or that they aren't the only person in the world feeling like this and that in fact there are millions of people feeling the same way as you are right now. Once you realise you are not alone in this, that you have discovered communities filled with 90x90 pixelated avatars representing people struggling in the same way you are, it can make the world seem that little bit bigger. Of course you need to interact with real humans too, you can't become an Internet-addicted weirdo who refuses to leave their keyboard and can't expose themselves to sunlight for fear of exploding into a cloud of ash, but from personal experience and from conversations I have had with other sufferers, creating your own digital support group can be a useful step towards preparing yourself for real-life interactions. It can, for want of a better expression, become cheap therapy.

DISCLAIMER: using the Internet is in no way a replacement for therapy and should not be treated as a cure or remedy for any mental health conditions you are suffering from. We've all looked up symptoms for a headache on the Internet and immediately thought we had a tumour the size of a small moon lodged in our think box; it works the same way with mental health. Self-realisation and diagnosis are two very different things. Thinking you have something wrong with you without any medical advice is realising you may have a problem. Telling your peers that you are a schizophrenic insomniac with telepathy without any of this being confirmed by a medical professional is a self-diagnosis, and ridiculous, and damaging to people really suffering from schizophrenic insomniac telepathy.

There are pros and cons when it comes to using the Internet when you are anxiously inclined. The pros being conversation, the normalisation of a condition brushed off to the side in normal society, research, education and being able to discuss a devastating disorder with brevity and humour, thereby making sufferers feel less alone and more in control of our own brains. The cons being that the Internet is the ultimate procrastination tool, and while you may have fully intended to log on and research Cognitive Behavioural Therapy at length to see if it was the right thing for you, after about three minutes you ended up on a website where dachshunds are dressed like little sailors and then sixteen hours have passed and for some reason you are trying to create a gif of sailor puppies re-en-acting the entirety of *HMS Pinafore* at 3 a.m. and you realise you haven't eaten in two days. In short, when your brain has a preference for ignoring reality, the Internet can exacerbate that problem.

I used the Internet as therapy. I used it as a distrac-tion from the real world. It wasn't an addiction, I just preferred it to normality. In real life there are people and bus accidents and random goose attacks, on the Internet there are just friends and followers, and news stories about bus accidents, and videos of random goose attacks, so it's definitely preferable. As I spent every night sat inches from a giant luminous square, one hand putting out a cigarette before lighting another, the other hand clutching a half and half rum and Coke, the other hand on a keyboa— wait.

I had replaced all feelings of anxiety with feelings of nothingness. I had taken socialising and attempting to face my problems and thrown them in a bin. And set that bin on fire. And then thrown the fire bin into a gorge. It was only when I veered away from the dog pictures and the forums on why the last season of *Lost* made absolutely no bloody sense that I discovered mental health communities, still very much in their infancy, but there they were. After my diagnosis this was one of my first experiences of speaking to anyone else with the same issues as me, and it felt . . . nice. People like me, with problems like me, in situations like mine, talking about it instead of hiding in a one-bed flat covered in cigarette ash and hummus. This is what inspired me to take getting help more seriously, to seek an answer as to why everyone else's brains worked one way and mine worked the other.

One of the key parts of 'getting better' is having a support group in place to help and assist you as you attempt to calm your brain down a bit. Support groups can appear in many different forms: your partner can be your support group; your mum or your dad, or both; your friends; your colleagues; a random person you met once in a bar and now you message occasionally. It can even just be a bunch of weirdos who you've never met who all live inside the Internet. To explore this further, I sat in a coffee shop in Camden and spoke to Ruby Elliot,* an artist and author, about her history with anxiety. Ruby discusses her own battles with her mental health on her blog (Rubyetc) and has helped thousands of people laugh about lives filled with mental illnesses. We spoke about the social aspects of anxiety and Ruby explained that in her teens she found herself unable to leave the house.

---

* She knew this was going to happen. I didn't just accost a woman trying to enjoy her morning coffee.

'I was pretty cut off due to my mental health issues, and as a result, my social circle has mainly come from being online. I think for some people who suffer from chronic mental health problems, this is not uncommon at all. I would say that I definitely lost some of my real-life friends due to my anxiety, but I found support online. The access to my support group was in my pocket. When you think about the social aspects of mental health, just the idea of Being Social can be paralysing, so with social media you can do it from the comfort of your own home. Most people with social anxiety find taking phone calls just as terrifying as speaking to people in public, but social media gives you access to something you thought you had lost and lets you feel less isolated. The feeling that you are not alone can be integral to recovery.'

Ruby explained that using social media actually helped her in her recovery and I have found this myself: the social aspects of social media are a sort of precursor to immersion therapy. The societal equivalent of trying a small shot of ale before committing to buying a full pint. Through social media you can learn to talk to people again, even if the conversations are via fingers and thumbs and brightly lit rectangles. It may not be as healthy as full immersion into a busy chaotic meeting in a public place but, for the anxious mind, it's better than sitting by yourself at home blocking out reality in all its forms. It all relates to a simple recovery rhetoric that will be repeated at you over and over: take one step at a time. Mine started like this:

'Don't write about your mental health! Why would anyone care that you are mental?'

'No one has to read it if they don't want to.'

'SO WHY WRITE IT THEN?'

'I feel better when I write.'

'Yeah and other people feel better when they take cocaine and punch clowns but you wouldn't recommend that they keep doing it.'

'It's not hurting anyone.'

'The clowns though?'

'Not that bit!'

'People will think you're weak. People will think you're as mad as a fish. No one will want to employ you or even befriend you if you talk about this.'

Despite my brain's protests, one of the best things I ever did in my life was to start writing about my mental health problems online. What fell out of my fingers into a keyboard was more eloquent and understandable than anything my mouth would ever allow. I found myself able to write about things I couldn't talk about. I found my outlet. Others have outlets like music, art, performance, sewing, masturbating on buses, stamp collecting. For me, I just wrote. I wrote blogs and saved them as drafts knowing I would never post them. I poured my mind into Word documents and saved them on USB sticks, and then placed the USB sticks into a *Raiders of the Lost Ark*-esque warehouse (a cheap cardboard folder I keep in my wardrobe).

Seeing my own thoughts, my own problems, my entire brain laid out in poorly spelt nonsensical ramblings in 11pt Helvetica made me feel better. It allowed me to quantify my madness and gave me a release that I hadn't found before. If you can find something – anything – that will shut up that tiny angry voice in your head for an hour or so, stick with it (as long as it's legal and not harmful, obviously). It's just self-care, a way to be nice to yourself. When your self is your own worst enemy, it will feel unnatural but, if you can, find something. Because when that tiny angry voice in your head does fade into the background, like someone trying to speak next to a helicopter in a movie, it's a wonderful thing. This can be Your Thing, you don't need to tell anyone about it, you don't need to share it on every social media stream you have, you can keep this tiny bit of yourself just for you, and be selfish with it. But if you are confident enough, or I suppose even stupid enough like I was, you can share it and I bet the results will not be what you expect.

Fuelled by a series of events that led me to evaluate my life choices in high definition, an unhealthy amount of cheap spiced rum and even cheaper Polish cigarettes I had bought under the counter at a dodgy corner shop, I hit send on a blog post. The first blog post I had ever written about my mental health. I say blog post, it was a long Tumblr post titled 'I think I might be crazy'. It was poorly written (yes even more poorly written than this book shut up), the grammar was all over the place, every other word was misspelt, in all honesty it was the nonsensical ramblings of a pissed-up twat that made about as much sense as listening to an audiobook with shuffle mode on. But I had written something and, while it was terribly conveyed, it was at least honest. I had not discussed my mental health with any of my friends or family. I hadn't acknowledged at any time previous to this that 'I am not OK', and this generally seemed like a fucking stupid idea.

But after half a bottle of rum and some terrible heavy metal where the lead singer sounds like a bear regurgitating an entire watermelon through a tuba, I thought 'Fuck it' and hit send. I expected no response, I expected a silent reaction, where people scrolled past it assuming I was just 'having a bad night' or someone had dumped me. It was 4 June 2011, I woke up the next morning with a hangover that felt like someone had poured a hot kettle of sambuca into my ears and then proceeded to beat me about the face with a ham in my sleep, and I checked my computer as I fumbled for my first cigarette of the day.

The response was unreal. People I had never spoken to, from walks of life I had never experienced, telling me how much they related to some words that had escaped from a rum-addled head box. I sat for hours reading the comments, the @ mentions, the direct messages, all from people who could relate to the story of a stranger. I didn't know how to respond. I typed and deleted 'Thank you?' a thousand times. After the replies calmed and I could focus, I replied to every single one individually and had conversations with people. I hadn't had conversations – proper conversations where there is a back and forth, not just them speaking and me nodding – in months. It was the first time I hadn't felt alone in a long time.

It's a selfish sensation, feeling alone when you have people around you – your family, your colleagues – but when you can't articulate the nonsense inside your own skull, you retreat and you find yourself alone. Through a keyboard I had found people I could talk to, and the risk of embarrassment was non-existent as I had time to find my words and responses. I didn't blurt out a reply in the hope of impressing someone, I articulated my thoughts until I was 100% happy with them. The inherent fear of socialising had been taken away, and while many may argue that talking via devices isn't actually socialising, I found it more comforting than any real conversation that I could have been involved in at the time.

The Internet has changed quite a bit since I started using it. What was once a novelty and a haven for the self-confessed weirdo is now a universal tool of conversation. Instead of having little pockets of the Internet to ourselves, we are now in a heaving crowd of idiots. What was once a relaxing pub with good music, cheap beer and polite conversation is now a strained speakeasy, serving the worst parts of humanity, with many of the patrons wearing disguises so as not to reveal their true selves, allowing them to be as crass and cruel as possible.

While my years on the Internet have left me rather

thick-skinned and accustomed to insults (people attempt to troll me on a daily basis, I have had two stalkers from the Internet and numerous – and bizarrely very real – death threats), the Internet did not play a huge part in raising me. My first interaction with the online world was trying to download a single Slipknot song via LimeWire and Kazaa, when to download a 3.5mb file took on average thirty to forty-five minutes as long as no one called the house phone.

Social media became a more prevalent part of my life in my early twenties, by which point I was pretending to be a functioning adult. The Internet and social media have definitely shaped parts of my personality but I hadn't used them during my teenage years, when experts say that all external stimuli have a profound effect on your psyche. In my twenties, coming as I did from a small, rural, predominantly white town, using social media educated me and opened my eyes to things that I never received through pub conversations and whatever bad newspapers I would find lying on the bar (I spent a lot of my 20s in pubs, leave me alone). After concluding that my time using the Internet in relation to my mental health had been predominantly a good experience (excluding the death threats, obviously), I became interested in how the younger generation uses social media, and if it has any effect on their mental health.

What I know about how young people use the Internet is just what I read. According to the *Daily Mail*, the only thing children use the Internet for is

Minecraft and sending pictures of their genitals to each other. According to other newspapers, every single person under twenty spends all their free time watching other people under twenty apply make-up on YouTube. This is tied in with the stereotypes that 'every young person is attached to their phones all the time' or 'kids are dumber now because all they care about are selfies and Snapchat', or 'every single child craves validation instead of working down the mine from the age of six'. While incredibly offensive, these do seem to be the general schools of thought for some of the older generations, mostly the ones who apparently spend most of their time sharing racist memes on Facebook. So to see how young people, mental health and the Internet actually mix, I had to do something that I tend to actively avoid . . . I had to speak to young people.

Off The Record (OTR) is a charity based in Bristol, a non-profit that works with young people in and around Gloucestershire who suffer with mental health problems. They speak to young people from all walks of life, with a large range of mental health problems, and the work they do has seen some amazing results in the people that go there. I first discovered OTR in 2015 when I co-founded a website called MindTank. The premise of the site was that people could write their own stories about mental health, and share them with other sufferers, sort of like a crowdsourced blog about mental health. Simon, the big boss of OTR, got in touch and wrote a piece for the site, and since then

I have been keeping an eye on all the work they have been doing. So I asked if OTR would mind if I bothered them for a day, and they were terribly kind and accepted. I met Liam (Head of Communications) and Simon at their offices. Simon explained the way the charity works: that anyone between the ages of eleven and twenty-five can come along and talk to OTR members about their problems. They offer a wide range of activities: sketch classes, painting, group therapy, one-on-one therapy. Whatever the mind needed – all things I didn't have access to at that age – it was taken care of by this charity. Liam then took me to a class called 'Mentality': a weekly after-school event where young people could go and discuss their issues in a safe, accepting environment. I was introduced as a 'guest speaker' and it was then that I realised that a man with severe anxiety exacerbated by public speaking was probably not the best person to be leading a discussion on the subject of anxiety. But we stuck with it.

I sat at the end of a series of grouped tables and listened as they talked among themselves. They were young people of different backgrounds, faiths, ages, who had come together by chance due to their mental health problems and their dedication to dealing with them in a healthy and profound way. Once again it showed me that mental health issues do not see the prejudices that people see; they're not selective. I sat making sure I had my questions ready, breathing heavily and trying to not let my sweat glands get the better of me. Liam introduced me and the entire class gave me a weary hello.

As with everything, I didn't mind a lack of expectation from them, as their low assumptions meant it was less likely that I would disappoint them. I choked my anxiety into my throat and began.

The first question I asked the group was the same one I asked everyone else I interviewed for the book, 'How would you define anxiety?' Yeah, I like to start small. They talked among themselves for a few minutes as I scribbled down notes on any passing comments I could hear. As the room quietened down, a young girl on the other side of the room from me raised her hand. 'I'm not sure how to define it, but it's basically making a bigger deal of something compared to how someone else would deal with it.' Yep. That's exactly it, I thought to myself. Next a young man raised his hand. 'Anxiety is a constant, I think people confuse being anxious and having anxiety. When you're anxious, that's only for a few minutes. But anxiety is always there.' Holy shit these guys were 'woke', as the kids say. Can I get away with saying that? No. No I can't. I won't ever say that again. I am so sorry.

The next person raised their hand. 'I think it's the battle between rational versus irrational. Some people deal with things in a rational way, when you have anxiety, you always go to the irrational way.'

Another hand went up: 'It's over-thinking a situation until it almost borders on paranoia. We take normal social situations and we blow every bad thing that could happen out of proportion.'

The purpose of that question was to make sure we

were all on the same page: anxiety can have so many definitions, and mean so many different things to people, and in all honesty, I had completely underestimated these guys. These guys were smart. A lot smarter than I was at their age.

Now, it's important to note here that I have not spent any time around young people for quite some time. I remember my own teenage years and, quite frankly, I was an idiot. When I was a teenager I thought *The Blair Witch Project* was a documentary, that wrestling was real, that I would grow up to be some sort of sexed-up spy who had a small veterinary practice on the side and that Limp Bizkit were at the forefront of a new musical revolution. I successfully failed all my A levels and I didn't even know what a selfie was, so personally I don't think the digital age has had a detrimental effect on young people, I just think that young people have always been demonised by older generations, and the digital revolution is just a new way to make the latter feel inferior. Anyway . . . !

I moved onto the next question: 'Do you think social media affects your mental health? Specifically, your anxiety.' They went away into groups and chatted among themselves. From the buzz in the room it appeared that they had a lot to say on this topic. I could have asked something simple, or gone to so-called social media experts (or 'gurus' or 'ninjas' or whatever they're calling themselves on LinkedIn nowadays) to get the answer, but what's easier than asking the community directly affected? You could also tell that OTR was a space where everyone was brutally honest. The first question was a good warm-up, but this is what I wanted to know. The first answer I received was:

'It's a support network, you have your friends, you have your people, in your pocket.'

This is exactly what I had hoped: a complete juxtaposition to the ideas the media feed us about how young people use the Internet. Surely the fact that young people had this resource, a resource that previous generations couldn't even imagine, is a positive thing? It broadens their minds with constant access to other people, to other human beings walking around on this planet with entirely different brain chemistry.

The next person spoke up:

'It's a way that I can express my thoughts in ways that I may not have been confident to do in public, it's a way to socialise in an extroverted way; you can be confident, you can have opinions.'

Once again, social media being used as an opportunity to achieve things that otherwise feel unachievable. Nothing wrong with that.

'I sometimes think people turn mental health into a competition. There have been times where I have tried to say that I am not doing very well, for instance, that I haven't been able to get out of bed for three days, and there will be someone else that will respond with, "well I once didn't get out of bed for six days".'

The room went silent with nods of agreement. Competitive mental health has been on the rise on social media for some time now. The next person responded:

'Some people seem to use their mental health problems as a badge of honour, and they've never even been to a doctor about it, they just think it's cool.'

People. Are. The. Worst. But this is a real problem that seems to be swept under the carpet in the mental health community. The bizarre thing is, many people see mental health problems as a quirk or a defining personality trait. I'm not sure if it's a narcissism thing, or just a matter of arrogance, but the last thing the mental health community needs is in-fighting. Saying to another sufferer that you have it worse than them so they shouldn't moan is the same as someone saying to someone with cancer, 'Cheer up, at least you're alive' – well, yes, but that's not very helpful. We discussed this concept for several minutes until I ran out of time. We briefly went over some other clichés of young people and social media. The majority said they mainly use it to speak to friends, that they don't follow that many celebrities and they don't aspire to live the perfect lives people display themselves as having on Instagram. The competitive comparability I found myself in seemed to be a generational thing. If anything, these young people knew that they were living their lives as best they could, and while social media had its problems, the feedback from them about it was mostly positive. For those afflicted with mental health disorders, it is a resource, an outlet, a way of testing the waters on the way to becoming a more extroverted person.

TIPS FOR A HEALTHY ONLINE EXPERIENCE:

⚡Talk

Your online persona is your own. You can use it however you want (as long as you're not being a dick – don't be a dick, we all have to suffer Donald Trump tweets every day already, and the world can only take so much fuckwittery). Converse, be supportive. If you see someone struggling, or you think they aren't doing so well, send a short message; you have no idea what that will mean to them. If you haven't got anything to say, read. Read other people's experiences and know you are not alone and there are millions of people who have written about their problems; you may just find a kindred spirit in a complete stranger. And if you still feel low, there are plenty of funny cat videos on YouTube.

⚡Don't read the comments

It seems like this has been a (not so) secret rule of the Internet for some time now. You only need to look at one *Daily Mail* comment section to find the worst in humanity. The Internet is like real life: those with the most ignorant opinions are usually the loudest. However, if you write something – anything – about your own experiences, read the comments. HYPOCRISY KLAXON. But for every troll, for every person trying to get a rise out of you, there will be a hundred people supporting you. Yes, the human brain is predisposed towards ignoring the positive and engulfing itself in the negative, but skip past them, delete them, mute them and read the positive ones over and over again like a mantra. The negative comments say more about them than you, always.

⚡Like your friends' selfies

A lot of people mock others for taking selfies and posting them online, but the fact of the matter here is that selfies don't hurt anyone. That person has taken a selfie because they feel good about themselves that day; a simple double tap or a like can help that person's self-confidence, let them know that someone out there is with them that day and digitally tell them: 'Hey, you look awesome today, you are doing awesome and KEEP BEING AWESOME GOD DAMN YOU!' . . . I got a bit carried away there but the message stands.

⚡Don't be a dick

Yes, it's easier to be mean than it is to be nice. Yes, we are currently living in some form of dystopian nightmare realm where nothing makes sense and the idiots are in charge, but don't go around looking for a fight. Looking at the Internet nowadays can be a roulette wheel of 'What am I pissed off about now?', but if you can post one nice thing, or just something that isn't feeding into the global hatred that day, you're doing well.

⚡Look after yourself, you dick

Self-care is as important online as it is in real life. Your online experience is your own, so don't put yourself through anything you wouldn't do in normal life. Avoid articles that could trigger any mental negativity, avoid tabloid websites, avoid self-diagnosis. Remember, for every bad thing on the Internet, there are thousands of nice things, there are people celebrating something worth smiling about, there are people spending their time making jokes for you to find funny, there are even Instagram accounts that are just pictures of piglets trundling around the place.

We all use the Internet differently: some of us can use it to help our mental health, some of us prefer to just play video games that mostly involve American teenagers announcing their intentions of seducing your mother, and some use it to watch other human beings enact very unhygienic practices upon one another – we are all different, but there is a little bit of hope out there.

10.
MY BRAIN VS. RESPONSIBILITIES

(AKA Gin Dinners, Exams And Gnome Theft)

We know from childhood that responsibilities are awful things. Clean your room. Do your homework. Brush your teeth. Stop breaking into the neighbours' garden and stealing the gnomes. OK maybe the last one is more about common sense and restraint than actual responsibility. As you get older your responsibilities alter. 'Clean your room' turns into 'keep your own house tidy because the mould on the plates in the sink has started to congeal into what could be defined as a brand new life form'. 'Do your homework' transforms into 'pay your bills, do your taxes, make sure you aren't falling into a pit of financial despair'. 'Brush your teeth' soon becomes 'book your own dentist appointments, make sure you wash or no one will ever love you, eat salad because otherwise you will die of plague or gout'. 'Stop breaking into the neighbours' garden and stealing their gnomes' turns into 'stop breaking into your neighbours' garden and stealing their gnomes'. You should have grown out of that by now.

'Are you going to pay that water bill today?'
'I can't, I haven't checked my bank balance in a few weeks and at this point I am entirely sure if I look at my balance it's just going to say the word NO in capital letters.'
'That's true, and if it says you have no money then you just have confirmation that you have failed as a human being.'
'Exactly.'
'OK, how about renewing the car insurance? Wait, that means you have to speak to people and you're fucking terrible at that.'
'Yep.'
'Maybe we should just accept that you are a catastrophe of a person and have a nap?'
'That's the first sensible thing you've said.'

We all see our lives going a certain way, and more often than not we deviate from our original plans and choose a path that is either more convenient, more profitable or that we are simply thrown into. Being a grown-up has its pros:

⚡Bedtime is whenever you want it to be.

⚡You can eat your lunch at 11 a.m. and no one can tell you otherwise.

⚡You can wear the same T-shirt three days in a row.

⚡You can just have gin by itself for dinner.

⚡You can go to any movies you want.

However, being a grown-up has a lot of cons too:

⚡You *could* go to bed whenever you want but if you do you'll just be tired the next day so it's probably a good idea to try to get an early night, I mean, it's 7 p.m. and you're yawning.

⚡You ate your lunch at 11 a.m. and now it's 3 p.m. and you feel like you're starving to death.

⚡You wore the same T-shirt for three days in a row and now all your friends are asking if you're OK and why you smell like a hedge covered in meat.

⚡You only had gin for dinner because you were too tired to make food and now you're just drunk and hungry and angry (drangry).

⚡The average cost of going to see a movie nowadays is about two weeks' rent and if you want popcorn you have to give over your firstborn child.

The real problem here is that we expect too much of ourselves. We expect that by the time we are twenty we will have life figured out, then we reach twenty-one and so push it to twenty-five . . . then thirty . . . and this continues until death. No one has life figured out. Maybe if we can control our responsibilities we can feel a little more in charge of our lives? Instead of feeling that we are constantly failing, we can feel that we are winning one small battle at a time. While life is a myriad of terrifying short stories it's also just lots and lots of tiny battles, battles you can win. The anxious mind is predisposed to negativity; we have covered this and I apologise for repeating myself, but it's important to remind yourself that while your brain is inventing new horrific scenarios and new reasons for you to feel like a failure, your brain is playing a trick on you. You're actually doing pretty well. Yeah you may not be doing *great*, you may not have a yacht, you may not be completely debt-free, you may have accidentally worn two non-matching shoes to work because you woke up a bit hungover from a dinner of gin and ran out of the house without checking, but you're not doing your absolute worst.

Being an adult can be divided into two different fields: Relaxation and Responsibility. Our time is split about 10% relaxation and 90% responsibility. I'm not including sleep as relaxation as it's a necessity: without sleep you just hallucinate and die. So you're responsible for making sure you have enough. God, it's just more pressure. We will discuss the stress of relaxation in the next chapter, as the anxious noggin doesn't want you to relax, it wants you to be worried, it wants you to be concerned, so relaxation can actually be incredibly taxing. To be able to relax we need to be able to put everything else into order, and that is where getting a handle on your responsibilities comes in. The main fight in anxiety is not overcoming anxiety. The main fight in anxiety is becoming you again. If you set your sights on simply banishing anxiety to the back of your mind you'll find it more difficult than trying to get through ordeals one at a time. But if you actually face up to it, and learn to cope, one step at a time, the end result will be taming your anxiety or, for lack of a better metaphor, hurling your foot into anxiety's nuts.

Avoidance behaviour is a common symptom of most forms of anxiety. It usually occurs after you've encountered an ordeal, seen it through but never want it to happen again. For example, if you were to have a panic attack in a bank, be it in a queue or at the till or checking your balance, your brain will remember every aspect of the situation that caused the panic attack. It's your brain trying to protect you again. So now you associate banks with panic attacks, and you feel panicky thinking about them, so you avoid them. Basically, you have accidentally taught yourself an emotional association. This can work with many situations, and while panic attacks are the most violent ways of your brain and your body reacting to an anxious situation, if you are feeling anxious, your brain will try to protect you by getting you out of there. It's fighting avoidance behaviour that is difficult. From dogs to children to adults (that's not an evolutionary chart, these are just examples – I'm almost positive dogs don't turn into children) we know that behaviour that is rewarded will be repeated. You give a dog a treat when it's good and it will want to be good again. Your brain is doing this to you with avoidance behaviour: when you avoid a stressful situation, your brain rewards you with a decrease in your anxiety, which we see as a positive, so we repeat our avoidance patterns. We are rewarding ourselves for being dickheads. Once again, anxiety makes little to no fucking sense. We've become so versed in this practice that we've given it a proper name. Procrastination. Take me writing this book for example:

'We should finish writing this.'
'But—'
'No come on now, we've only got a thousand words to do and then we can take a break.'
'But—'
'Come on.'
'Let's do the washing-up instead!'
'Why?'
'Because it's not this.'

Procrastination is brilliant. I have genuinely no idea how I finished this book! It's almost an art form unto itself. It's more than likely that some of the most important discoveries and most brilliant pieces of art were created during bouts of avoiding something that was much more important at the time. I for one can imagine da Vinci painting the *Mona Lisa* because he was avoiding doing his tax return. My bouts of procrastination are nowhere near as culturally significant, but before writing this chapter of the book I cleaned the house, alphabetised my DVD collection, organised my sock drawer and spent fifteen minutes watching YouTube tutorials of how to properly descale a kettle. I may be behind schedule on writing but goddammit the kettle looks fucking amazing.

TIPS ON HOW TO AVOID PROCRASTINATION:

⚡Imagine all of your dead relatives have surrounded you and are looking upon you in shame.

⚡Set goals throughout the day and choose small rewards upon accomplishing said goals. You know how you train dogs to shake hands and stop eating the sofa? It's like that, apart from you are the dog now because you have no self-control.

⚡Convince yourself everything has a deadline and that you are only ever an hour away from that deadline so you need to complete the task as soon as humanly possible and stop titting around.

⚡In all honesty I think the shame ghost people might be the best option here.

We've all experienced procrastination at some point in our lives, be it that time we went out drinking to avoid studying for an exam, or that time we rearranged all the books in our house into order of cover colour just so we didn't have to answer an important text message. It's a fault we are all guilty of and it's not laziness, it's a psychological defence mechanism. HA. In your face anyone who ever said I was lazy! However, this justification for avoiding tasks that other humans find easy doesn't stand up in reality. You can't say to your boss: 'Yes, I know that the deadline was 4 p.m. but my brain was trying to protect me from something it perceived as a negative in my life so instead I organised the stationery cupboard.' Procrastination is a great way to temporarily avoid things, but inevitably we must meet our chores head-on. This is just another example of how being a responsible grown-up is boring, but there are ways to beat this. As with most anxiety-related dilemmas, it involves small steps and taking yourself out of your comfort zone. As I said, we aren't here to kill anxiety, we are here to tame it.

FINANCES

I have tried to be as honest as I can in this book, as from a young age I was told that honesty is the best policy, and in my teens Professor Umbridge in the Harry Potter series told me 'I must not tell lies', so I will be brutally honest here: I am fucking terrible with money. If a bill comes through the post I have an existential crisis, and I approach checking my bank balance with the same fear and wariness that someone would approach a furious mountain gorilla wielding a machete. (The gorilla has the machete, where would it even get a machete? Wait, I think I've seen this film.) I've had panic attacks when my cards have been declined, I've come out in sweats when told that a company would need to do a credit check on me. I convince myself that said credit check would reveal my (imaginary) sordid financial past. I imagine that I won't be able to get a new phone contract because of that time my account went over its overdraft because I drunk-bought Wolverine's leather jacket off eBay.* As a result of my own ineptitude in this field I am not going to become a financial guru. I am not going to tell you to 'invest in melons' or 'buy shares in cats' or whatever those things mean. I am just going to relay some of the things that keep me sane when dealing with money.

1. Keep lists

Lists are fucking brilliant when dealing with anxiety. You can quantify your problems and concerns in a tangible way. Checking off a completed task on a list also gives you a sense of achievement; be it a small task like 'had a shower today' or 'didn't murder anyone', these little victories are an invaluable weapon in your anxiety-

---

* To clarify, the jacket worn by the *X-Men* character Wolverine, not a jacket made by wolverines or made of tiny wolverines oh God that sounds horrible.

beating arsenal. I don't mean to be patronising, but keep a log of all your outgoings and incomings, make sure you know where all your money is coming from and going to – this will give you a sense of control that may have been lacking in your addled think kettle.*

2. Check your fucking balance

OK this one does sound patronising. I apologise for nothing. It also sounds a lot easier than it is. You don't have to do it every day, you don't have to subject yourself to a thorough scrutiny of your entire financial history, but it's good to know where you are at the moment. Check your bank balance when you get paid. This might be on a monthly basis or when an invoice has been paid, but take a little look and just confirm to yourself that your work is paying off. The fuel that feeds the fire of anxiety is uncertainty; any form of uncertainty allows your befuddled brain to invent scenarios and play with your paranoia.

3. Save money but treat yo' self

All the bank adverts tell us: 'If you don't save money you will die.' It is important to know that if you do not have savings, you will not instantly perish, you're just a bit further away from buying a boat than other people. Basically, try to have a rainy-day fund, keep enough

---

* There are plenty of apps that can help you do this, because of course there are. There are apps for everything, there is probably an app that tells you how disappointed your father is with you at any one time.

money squirrelled away to sort out your taxes when you need to, but don't go bananas. You don't have to become one of those coupon people you see on the TV who manages to get a monthly shop for 20p but spends twenty-four hours a day cutting out tiny bits of paper from magazines they found in the woods; just save enough so you can maybe go on holiday in the future. It doesn't have to even be a massive holiday, you don't need to go to the Maldives and Instagram your fabulous lifestyle, diving with octopi and giving yourself champagne enemas or whatever it is travel bloggers do, you can just go on a small city break for a few days, or even just the countryside for a long weekend. It's clichéd but remember, you don't live so you can work, you work so you can live.

SOCIAL RESPONSIBILITIES (AKA 4,000 WEDDINGS AND A FUNERAL)

There comes a stage in life that every adult secretly fears, secretly loathes and secretly hopes will never come round again, and that is wedding season. As you soar past your mid-twenties your friends start panic-marrying people, and you are invited to watch. Weddings are obviously happy occasions: two human beings have given up shopping around for mates and have settled on the one with the least awful qualities of all the people who were available at the time. To celebrate this, they pay horrendous amounts of money so you get the opportunity to get pissed and dance to Will

Smith's 'Gettin' Jiggy Wit' It' and fall over, taking out the mother of the bride. It's a beautiful event.

Then your friends start having babies, and you have to meet the tiny screaming versions of people you used to go drinking with who now don't stop talking about nappies and pooping. Then people start dying, because people are selfish and have a tendency to do that, so you have to go to funerals, which are a bloody awful practice. Social responsibilities obviously don't mix well with social anxiety – that goes without saying at this point – but unfortunately some occasions are a necessity to attend and, while it can be taxing, this gives us the opportunity to shove our hard work in anxiety's face. These events do lend themselves to things the anxious brain is predisposed to find difficult: socialising, socialising with strangers, public speaking, even at times being the centre of attention. These are all things we can handle, if we prepare for them properly. We analyse potential threats, we go over them, we beat them.

Socialising and socialising with strangers

When you are seated at a wedding you are usually put onto a table with that one guy you recognise from school, his girlfriend, a person you don't know and two older people who look thoroughly uncomfortable with the entire situation. You are now forced friends through proximity, you must get to know these people for some reason. The average wedding introduction conversation with people you've just met goes something like this:

'Hello, and how do you know the happy couple?!' you ask with as little apathy as possible.

'Well I used to be Brendan's dentist when he was five, and this is my sixteenth wife, Gertrude.'

'Oh.'

'It's a funny story how we met let me tell you at length . . .'

'Oh no thank you, this interaction is over.'

We are back to our faking-it tutorial. Small talk can be difficult. Your brain wanders. With every little bit of information you give out about yourself you panic: 'Is this important? This person obviously doesn't care. Do I sound like a tit saying this?' If you find yourself in a small-talk situation that is causing you physical pain just ask questions. Keep the conversation flowing without actively being a part of it; you can join in later if the time feels right, or you can simply be the orches-trator of other people's dialogue. If you get to a stage where it's all becoming too much, excuse yourself for a moment, get some fresh air, collect your thoughts and talk your anxious brain off that cliff. The nice result of the faking-it technique is that soon it becomes second nature and you're not faking it any more, you are just being you.

HOW TO SURVIVE A WEDDING WITH AN ANXIOUS BRAIN 101:

⚡Take someone you trust with you as your plus one.
Let this person know how you're feeling, ask this

person to be your safety blanket, ask them to let you know if you are rambling or have had sixteen bottles of wine and are doing the Funky Chicken during the best man's speech.

⚡**Know your exits.** You can always ask to be seated near the door, or with people you know, whatever gives you any sense of calm.

⚡**If you are asked to do a speech and don't want to do a speech, don't do a speech.** There will be dozens of drunken well-wishers who would give their left nipple to boozily say how much they love the couple. It's another rule of anxiety, don't let anyone put you in a position that makes you uncomfortable.

⚡**Don't worry about how everyone else is doing, worry about how you are doing.** Actually this is a good rule for life. That would make a good motivational quote. Put a Minion next to it and it's basically Facebook gold.

PUBLIC SPEAKING

Public speaking is horrible. Speaking is horrible. Being in public is horrible. Everything is horrible. End of sub-chapter.

. . . Fine, I'll go on.

Fear of public speaking is common among anxiety sufferers. It is out of our comfort zone, it puts us in a vulnerable place where we are open to criticism, critique, and humiliation. It is a situation we would try to protect ourselves from at all costs. However, it can be difficult to get out of a public speaking engagement if, say, you have been made best man at your friend's wedding, or you've written a book on anxiety and now have to promote it (OH GOD). We try to find any excuse we can to get out of it, but we have to suck it up. The best way I have found to deal with this is practice. 'Practice makes perfect', the expression goes, but I think it should be something along the lines of 'Practice makes perhaps-I-won't-throw-up-in-front-of-a-room-full-of-people-this-time.' When I started CBT one of the things I wanted to deal with was speaking in public. My previous encounters with public speaking went something along the lines of:

1. Get words wrong
2. Sweat through clothes
3. Mumble under my breath
4. Forget I can't swear in this situation and swear my tits off at being annoyed with myself
5. Self-loathing
6. This pit of self-loathing isn't deep enough
7. Make pit of self-loathing deeper
8. The pit of self-loathing has no escape and now I live in the pit please forward my mail to the pit

If you find yourself in the position of having to throw your words out of your face into a room full of people, try the following: write your speech in its entirety, don't leave room for ad libbing, get some people you trust (your family, your friends, a partner, your pet even) and read it aloud to them over and over again until you feel confident. Let them critique you, let them help you, and do this until you feel that you can deliver a speech with the confidence of a Welsh weather reporter about to say Llanfairpwllgwyngyllgogerychwyrndrobwllllantysiliogogogoch.

EDUCATION

'If you fail this exam, your future is ruined. You will never get a job, you will never find love, you will die alone, with no money, having lived your days in a bin, your only friend being a raccoon that once robbed you at knifepoint.' Not that we put too much pressure on students or anything. We are now even at a point where society has put so much pressure on students that an entire generation is overqualified for most jobs going. We ingrain a fear of failure into human beings as young as four: 'You can't get this test wrong because it means you're stupid if you do', 'You can't fail this exam because that's just throwing your future away', 'You can't take seventeenth-century pornographic doodling at university because that's a useless skill.'

Young people have a crap time of it, really. If it's not the stress of school, it's the worry of social status, the low levels of self-esteem, the expectations thrust upon them by an over-expectant society, the critique of their lifestyle by older generations. Yep, being young is hard. If you're a young person read this next bit carefully: failing your exams is not the end of life as you know it. You aren't going to die alone. You haven't thrown away your life. Maybe tests just aren't your thing? Maybe your knowledge lies outside of constantly changing curriculums. This is not to say that you shouldn't care about your exams/homework/extra-curricular activities, it just means the pressure that is being put onto you to be perfect is unjustified and unreasonable. Sorry to be rude, but you'll never be perfect, because you are human. Pressure like this leads to fear and fear leads to uncertainty, and with a mind filled with uncertainty, panic, unjustified expectation, fear, how are we supposed to operate at 100%? If we take those negatives away, if we can approach any situation with a reasonable perspective – not even confidence, just perspective – we take away the control this situation has over us.

It's rational thinking versus irrational thinking again, another symptom of the anxious brain. The rational side of your brain is quiet, reasonable, he's the guy in the pub sat by himself reading a book with half a pint of Guinness. The irrational part of your brain is loud, stupid, he's the guy stood at the bar by himself getting loaded on Strongbow and black and constantly whistling at the barmaid. Everyone in the pub hates him, he's causing chaos and ruining this evening for everyone, but because he is the loudest and most obnoxious, all eyes are on him, and not the quiet guy reading his book in the corner. The point is, you have to stop paying attention to the bit of your brain making the most noise, and try to listen to the sage advice buried underneath. The irrational part of your brain is screaming that if you fail an exam you are throwing your future away, but the rational part of your brain will be quietly trying to tell you that you can just do your best, that that's the most anyone can expect of you and that if you fail, you fail. You can retake a test, you can resit an exam, breathe.

The fight between the irrational and the rational is another in the long list of battles the anxiety-riddled among us have to endure; however this battle can help us with avoidance behaviour too, and the route to controlling this is through hindsight. If we fuck up once, we tell ourselves we aren't going to do it again. While avoidance will analyse the situation as a threat, if we can employ hindsight it allows us to analyse the event and identify the triggers. For example, you fuck up an exam. Do you?

A - Avoid any future situations that may involve an exam, application form or any variation of testing, reluctantly accepting your new life as someone who lives off the grid, unemployable, uneducable, a maverick of anonymity, an undoc-umented renegade.

B - Look back on the event, identify the problems that led to negative impressions of the experi-ence, and help your brain rewire itself to not address any similar situations as threats.

It's like a choose-your-own-adventure book but for people who are predisposed to self-destructive lifestyles.

We suffer from predictable anxiety and unpredictable anxiety. With unpredictable anxiety, yep, you've guessed it, its very nature is unpredictable, so it is difficult to find a trigger that causes an attack (like having a random panic attack and never figuring out what the fuck caused it). Once again, our bodies are just dicks sometimes. But with predictable anxiety we can identify a cause. You had a panic attack in the queue at the post office? Was it too busy? Next time we'll try going when it's quieter: easy! You had a panic attack before an exam? Had you put a lot of pressure on yourself beforehand? Next time, give yourself a fucking break. Don't cram studying into the night before the test, don't put all your eggs in this basket, as it were (how many eggs do you need to buy on a weekly basis to justify carrying them in a basket?) and don't do yourself any psychological damage over something that you can approach again.

We are all guilty of overworking ourselves, trying to live up to self-imposed responsibilities until we eventually break and can't do it any more. It's called burning out. There is only so much stress you can put your own body and mind through before the system overloads. To return to a previous analogy, you have too many tabs open on a web browser and it will crash, and your brain is the same way.

FAMILY

It's seven years ago and I'm sat in the garden of my in-laws' house, my wife's father has just cooked a BBQ and we are about to tuck in. It's my first time of meeting her parents properly, I was trying to be on my best behaviour. I didn't want, at any point, for this guise of a perfectly normal human being who was a suitable candidate for their daughter's affection to fail. I even ironed a shirt. I was all over it. 'What are you working on at the moment?' my mother-in-law asked. I burst out laughing, not a sincere laugh, a manic laugh, like something a supervillain would do just after dispatching one of his henchmen with a harpoon. Why did I laugh like a hyena on poppers? I have no idea. I panicked. I panic-laughed. Who the fuck panic-laughs?

Family life comes with all sorts of different responsibilities. Making sure your parents don't think you're wasting your life, looking after siblings, looking after children, meeting the in-laws. Yep, it's another anxiety minefield! In an attempt to avoid repeating myself I will skip the awkward interactions with in-laws and distant relatives, as the same rules apply here as they do with any form of social anxiety. Instead, I'm interested in how the dynamics of family gel together with the anxious brain.

I spoke to Mia Vaughan again, of Cigarettes and Calpol, as she writes brilliantly about managing anxiety with a daughter. I wondered how the dynamic of anxiety and motherhood together works for her – I know how hard it is just to look after myself, let alone a tiny hyperactive version of me running around the place

My first question was, 'How does parenthood impact your anxiety?' Mia said:

'In a lot of ways being a parent has meant that I can't let myself wallow or fall too far into an anxiety spiral. I have to pull myself out of it because this tiny person is not only watching and learning from me but completely relying on me to keep her alive. I have to drag myself to the shops to make sure there's food in for dinner, I have to make that phone call to the doctor's, I have to fill out that stack of forms for school placements, I have to talk to the other mums at the school gates. There's a lot of ways that being a parent pushes you to do things you could otherwise hide from. Mental illnesses are inherently selfish, that's just how they work, so when you have somebody else relying on you there has to be – to some extent – less of that.

'It does of course also mean the guilt of having a Bad Day is a thousand times worse. If you can't face public transport so cancel drinks with a friend you feel bad, but if you can't face public transport and cancel a day out your child has been desperate for you feel like the worst person on the planet. You want to do everything for that small person and when some days you just can't, you feel like you're letting them down. Mum guilt is something being written about by mummy bloggers across the world, it's a phenomenon that no matter your circumstance you experience to some

213

degree, so add in a nice dose of debilitating mental illness and you've got yourself the perfect ingredients for a cocktail of guilt like no other.'

While anxiety itself is a burden, for Mia having a child had seemingly created a level of certainty within life that could temporarily expel negativity, and create focus, drive, a goal to work towards. From what I could gather, it made it seem like aspects of parenthood inadvertently worked as immersion therapy for her. My next question was a bit harder. 'What is your daughter's understanding of anxiety?'

'I don't think parents should hide all their emotions from their children. While they don't need to see you at your absolute worst – red, snotty, unable to catch your breath – I think it is important for children to understand that adults have emotions and feelings too. Empathy is something we're never too young for.'

My first thought here was: 'I really need to stop interviewing people for this book who are more eloquent than me.' I wrote back, 'What tips do you have for others with anxiety, particularly for those with children?'

'I think the most important thing for all of us is to be a little gentler with yourself. We are so often programmed to believe that anxiety is just a symptom of modern life or something we should be able to get over. This isn't the case! As with any illness, sometimes you need time to rest and recuperate; you have to allow yourself this with a mental illness too. Don't make yourself feel bad for not conquering the world today, sometimes it has to wait until tomorrow.

'It can be easier said than done to take time to rest when you're a parent, especially if you're a lone parent, but take it where you can. Take up that offer from a family member or friend to take them out for the day, order the food shop online, stock the freezer with ready meals. Despite what that mum on Instagram says, you don't need to spend every minute filling water bottles with glitter and cooking vegan, sugar-free Colin the Caterpillars from scratch (unfollowing that mum on Instagram is a good tip too). Kids are simple and adaptive, they're just as happy lying in bed, eating pizza and reading books as they are on an immersive, educational day at the organic farm. We all want to provide the best life for our children, but nobody has ever succeeded at doing that while driving themselves to a breakdown due to a lack of self-care. Look after yourself and it will be easier to look after them.'

A parent/child relationship is obviously a very dependent one, but the feeling of duty and responsibility lives within most family relationships – we all want to be the best we can be for the people we love, we all want to contribute to a healthy and happy family dynamic. Living with anxiety isn't easy, at no point is anyone ever going to tell you it is, but if you can find your coping mechanisms, your comfort blankets, and if you give yourself a fucking break, you can make life that little bit easier for yourself. Your takeaway from this interaction may be very different from mine, but to me it's that a source of consistency and responsibility can have positive effects on the anxious mind.

Having someone depend on you is a challenge unto itself, whether it's a child, a sibling or even a friend. Add anxiety into the mix and it can start to feel like a lot of pressure, and you'll need to find your own ways of coping.

It's one of the key things to remember when it comes to taming an anxious mind: we all have our struggles, we all have things going on we wish we could forget about, or that someone else could worry about them for us, but we need to look after ourselves in whichever way we feel comfortable with. Once again, there is no playbook, no manual or tutorial; you need to identify your own ways of finding your peace of mind.

Unless you can afford to hire someone to carry you everywhere, pay all your bills for you and give you a back rub while spoon-feeding you cake, then you're going to have to look out for yourself. The anxiously inclined are susceptible to bouts of self-destruction. Unfortunately, it's easier to not look after yourself than it is to look after yourself. It's easier to have gin for dinner than it is to cook a meal. It's easier to avoid paying your bills than it is to pay them. It's easier to get stressed over an exam than to approach it calmly. Training your brain to approach situations in a new light is extremely difficult, there's no sugar-coating it, but you are trying and trying is a massive fucking step away from doing nothing. As we discussed with avoidance behaviour, if we feel rewarded – with a lack of anxiety for example – we want to repeat the action that made that possible, so if we can tackle a problem (say we cooked a meal for ourselves instead of inhaling a litre of gin) we deserve a reward, we deserve to relax, and that takes us to our next chapter.

11.
MY BRAIN VS. RELAXATION

(AKA Sneezing Fits, Crab Walks and Breathing)

Right. We've got up, we've left the house, we've done our commute and we've survived another day at work. It's time for some downtime. It's time to relax. If you make the hamster run in his wheel constantly, without breaks, without sleep, he dies. The hamster is your brain. The wheel is you. No, wait, that makes no sense. The wheel is your brain. The hamster is you. Fuck, this is just a terrible analogy. Maybe we are all the hamster? Oh God I am too deep into this poorly constructed metaphor to dig my way out. Society is the wheel. No. Fuck. Let's start again.

'OK, it's time to relax.'
'But . . . the things . . .'
'What things?'
'And the stuff.'

'What stuff?!'
'THE THINGS AND THE STUFF.'

Modern life is busy, fast, unrelenting and cruel. No one has it easy, apart from maybe people who have lots of money and nice things and a milkshake robot that follows them around constantly dispensing milkshakes. (Note for later, file patent for milkshake robot.) The only person who is going to make sure that you are doing OK is you, and, I am going to repeat myself again, you need to give yourself a fucking break. When your brain is going 100 miles per hour at every moment of your existence it can be increasingly difficult to tell it to pause, or if not that, just go a little bit slower for a bit.

Personal question, and think about this for a moment, when was the last time you felt truly relaxed? I mean properly relaxed, where you weren't thinking about responsibilities, you weren't worrying in the back of your mind – when was the last time your brain felt like it was in standby mode? I think I have been relaxed, by which I mean 'properly not thinking about anything properly properly' relaxed, twice in my life. The first when I was reading a book in a pool on my honeymoon, but then I fell asleep and almost drowned and ruined my book, and the second was when I treated myself to a massage. The massage was all going well, but then when the masseuse started laying into my back I, for some reason unbeknownst to me, muttered, 'THAT'S THE BADGER.' I haven't had a massage since, and now don't trust myself around bodies of water.

Let's start this chapter as we mean to go on: make yourself a nice cup of tea, or coffee (if you haven't had 6,000 already today), or get yourself a glass of wine or a beer if the time is appropriate (if not just claim it's your birthday, I think that's allowed) and chill out for a bit.

You're more than likely aware that telling an anxious brain to relax is like whispering 'Can everyone just calm down a bit?' in the middle of a full-scale riot. Self-care is a key element to taming your anxiety, it goes hand in hand with your choices of medication and/or therapy, it's impossible to start feeling like you again unless you do the things you want to do. That's what we are doing here isn't it? Trying to get back to feeling somewhat like ourselves again. As machines of worry we keep ourselves constantly beavering away, trying to solve one task at a time, be those physical or emotional tasks, and we're constantly preoccupied, our anxiety guiding us down different paths of fear. I'm speaking for myself, though I'm sure you can relate in some way, but when I actually sit down at the end of a bloody long-hour day, open a beer and put my feet up, my brain instantly shouts: 'Well if you're relaxing it means we've obviously forgotten to do something, we've missed something integral. Quickly, let's go through everything that we could have forgotten today!' We are so in tune with worry that when we have nothing to worry about, we worry because we aren't worrying. Isn't the human brain wonderful?*

Personally, I have developed three different ways to force my brain into an induced form of tranquillity: the redirection method, the rewarding method and the required method. It's important to say at this point that this is not based in any form of science, this is straight out of my own personal cranium circus, but they are ways that I have found helpful. Redirection is the act of simply distracting yourself in such a way that anxiety has to really try bloody hard to creep in. Rewarding is a forced way of getting the correct chemicals going to the correct places by doing things you enjoy, and required are things you should do regardless, things that will add to your arsenal of anxiety-fighting weapons. So here is a list of things you can do to help your anxious mind relax, some ideas to take away to fit into your schedule for self-care and self-love (not that type of self-love; don't be gross, or be gross, do what you want).

DISCLAIMER: These might sound patronising, again, and well . . . they kind of are, but we are all idiots and need a good push in the right direction.

---

* This is a rhetorical question, the brain is a complete twat. We've been through this SEVERAL TIMES now.

THE REDIRECTION METHOD

We've all been in a situation where we try desperately to change the topic of conversation as quickly as we can. A family member has started talking about another family member while that family member is in the room. It's awkward. No one is saying anything. Your drink is empty. Even the cat is looking like it's trying to think of an excuse to leave. What's the normal reaction? 'SO ANYONE GOING ANYWHERE NICE ON HOLIDAY SOON?' you scream to try to defuse the situation. This is what we are doing here, we are creating a deliberate distraction; yes it's less than subtle, but hey we are a bunch of bananas people, simple works for us. So here are my redirection techniques of choice:

1. Exercise.

Yep. I said it. A word so dirty I feel like I have to take a Brillo pad to my brain for merely uttering it. You will hear a lot about exercise being a saving grace for the mentally ill, some even talk about it like it's a cure – it's not a cure, but it is redirection, it's focus and it's sweaty and annoying. And it *can* help. Not only for the obvious reasons (making you healthier) but for your self-esteem, self-confidence and self-worth, and because while you're panting away on a running machine like a bulldog eyeing up a steak, your main focus is 'OH JESUS FUCK I HATE THIS OH GOD MY LEGS HURT OH SWEET MERCIFUL FUCK I CAN'T FEEL MY

SKIN' and your anxiety is squished to the back of your brain, temporarily silenced by sweat and swearing. You don't have to become one of *those* gym people, you don't have to post a selfie of you looking like you've been mauled by a cloud of sweat and terror, you don't have to check in every time you go on Facebook so all your friends who are neck-deep in curries at the exact same time feel awful about themselves; you are doing it for yourself. You don't have to push yourself, you don't have to get a personal trainer or go every single day for seventeen hours, you just do what you feel comfortable with.

You also don't have to go to a gym, you don't even have to go for a run: go for a long walk, walk the dog, get your blood flowing and your muscles working and knock your anxiety on its arse. By doing exercise we are increasing our levels of serotonin in these meat husks we call bodies, so our balance of chemicals becomes somewhat more regular. Of course, adrenaline is pumping through you like porridge through a wind tunnel (nope, no idea what that means) but with the added neurotransmitters and hormones our body regulates where the blood flow needs to go, unlike the body's reaction to a panic attack where it just makes everything a messy nonsense. Some anxiety sufferers claim that exercise is better than any therapy or medication they've ever had. Of course, what works for some doesn't work for all, and as I am a grumpy sod, here is a list of things I think are wrong with all things exercise:

⚡ If humans were supposed to swim we wouldn't drown all the time

⚡ Cycling is just sitting down with an added inconvenience

⚡ Times you should have to run. 1 – A bear is chasing you. 2 – You are chasing a bear because it has stolen your picnic basket

⚡ All sports are just an extended game of 'Get that thing over there' and go on for hours

⚡ If humans were supposed to lift weights our backs wouldn't break so easily

⚡ Rowing is just swimming but cheating

⚡ Everyone who finds lifting weights fun has probably shouted something mean out of a van

⚡ The only sport worth watching or doing is that one where they all wear fancy suits and get horses to dance

2. Meditation

The second thing we can do to direct our minds away from anxious inklings is to meditate. When I hear the word meditation I think of a man in a silky tangerine gown perched atop a mountain communing with nature in an attempt to transcend his human form and finally become a being of pure energy. Just me? OK. Meditation isn't just the hippy-dippy stuff we see in the movies. In all fairness, if I had to sit cross-legged for more than five minutes at any one time, my legs would go numb and I would now just have to live in the position I had locked myself into, shuffling myself around on my hands like a crab. If you can cross your legs without giving yourself a hernia then be my guest, cross your legs at all times, on the tube, at christenings, in the supermarket queue, go for it. If you are more inclined to try something a little bit more personal, there are loads of apps that help with guided meditations.

Guided meditation usually involves an American with an accent that sounds like it's fallen straight out of a reality TV show about housewives who have to blow up the moon (I don't watch that much American TV, sorry), who gargles instructions into your ears through your phone. For example: 'Relax. Close your eyes. If you are sitting down, put your hands on your lap, if you are lying down, get up, this exercise doesn't work like that. Now, imagine you are a baby monkey, in a basket made of fluffy things, floating down a river. Maybe the river is filled with piranhas? Maybe it's filled with the souls of your enemies. As you are floating you can hear the scream of the rhinoceros shark chasing after you, what do you do? NOTHING. IT HAS YOU. IT HAS YOUR BABY MONKEY ARM IN ITS SHARKY GOB. STOP THIS MEDITATION NOW.'

OK, sarcasm aside, it can help. Put your headphones

on, pick a guided meditation and listen to Chet from Orange County tell you how to survive today. Just listening to someone else's voice and having something to concentrate on while you focus on your breathing can be monumentally helpful, and a great way to prepare you for another venture into your daily grind. If you are feeling brave give yoga a go too, if only to teach your body how to handle breathing properly. We will get on to the importance of breathing techniques in a bit, but meditation and yoga can be invaluable in helping you regulate your breath. The practices you can learn through these two activities can be used in situations of panic – who thought yoga could be helpful? The Hindus and Buddhists I guess. Damn it. Do monks suffer with panic attacks? We should probably move on.

3. Education

Last but not least of our distracting activities is the simple task of educational enlightenment. We've got to keep cramming our heads with new stuff; it's the only way we can grow as human beans. We have to keep our minds stimulated or they will perish, falling apart like a croissant in a dishwasher. In simple terms, your brain is a houseplant, yeah it may be useless but if you don't water it it dies and leaves a godawful smell hanging around the place. One of the symptoms of anxiety can be apathy. But this is also a symptom of growing up: we get lazy, we are busy all the time, we are tired all the time, putting any form of effort into something new can be an immense task. But expanding your mind doesn't need to be taxing; it can often occur without you even knowing it, because brains are stupid and make no sense. (Also by 'expanding your mind' I mean in an intellectual way not in a 'let's do this postage stamp of drugs until our skin feels like gravy' sort of way.)

HERE ARE SOME EASY WAYS TO KEEP YOUR BRAIN ACTIVE:

⚡**Read books.** Books are like movies but you get to invent what the character looks like and if you hate the ending you just set fire to it.

⚡**Write.** Writing is when words come out of your fingers and if you're anything like me it's usually terrible, but it can be extremely therapeutic. No one else has to read it, just sit for a while and write whatever comes to your mind, it can be a blog about your day or fan fiction about Dumbledore falling in love with Mario and going on holiday to Venice and Mario proposes as they are taking a gondola ride,* it's completely up to you.

⚡**Open your ears.** Music, podcasts, audiobooks, all are good for your brain. Find things that interest you:

* This idea is already copyrighted, don't even THINK about stealing it. If there are any film studio execs reading, get your people to call my people, yeah?

pancakes, dictators, grasshoppers – whatever you're interested in, there will be something to ram into your ears.

⚡ **Create.** Make your own music, paint your own art, write your own scripts. Your mind is capable of some amazing things so give it a go, you might be completely and utterly shit at it, but keep going. For instance, Van Gogh's first painting was a stick figure drawing of a donkey (this may not be true).

⚡ **Learn a new skill.** Ever wanted to speak Japanese? Fuck it, learn it, what's stopping you? A restraining order against the whole of Japan? OK that's fair enough, but if that is not the case what have you got to lose, you can learn it at home and never have to bother another human soul with it. Learn a new language, learn to juggle, learn to bake a cake, it's up to you, take an hour once a day and see how it goes.

⚡ **Get your ass back to school.** Ever felt like you didn't get the most out of your education? Fail every subject like I did? Then don't worry! You're not subject to a life of grim unemployment, you can go to a marvellous thing called NIGHT SCHOOL. Night school is great because everyone there is over twenty-one and has an addiction. In all seriousness, a course can be very enriching if new qualifications will give you a better CV and also give you drive that you may have been lacking.

⚡ **Learn how to speak to dogs.** Please do this, then teach me how to, it must be possible.

THE REWARDING METHOD

Not everything you do to help your anxiety has to be geared towards teaching yourself to overcome something. Some things you can do just because you like to do them. Our interests will usually be as individual as our fingerprints, or as individual as our weird laughs after a bottle of red wine. (Mine is the honk, loud piercing honks, it's terrible.) I say this a lot in this book, but you need to give yourself a fucking break. You can tell there is a 'but' coming can't you? It's got to that point where you can tell when I'm going to be patronising again, sorry about that. *ahem* BUT, we have to make sure these things are good for us, good for our minds and good for our, if you believe in the concept, souls. So what follows in this weird section are some ideas for ways to find a sense of calm more because you feel like you've earned it rather than anything distractionary.

1. Food
Let's start with food. Healthy food leads to a healthy mind. Bollocks. BOLLOCKS I SAY. Food is love. Food is life. My body is a temple, but it's full of chicken

nuggets and it's better than most temples because the other ones aren't filled with chicken nuggets. That's my stance on this and I am sticking to it. A lot of mental health writers are advocates for clean eating, smoothies made from bushes and despair, and diets so confusing that if you accidentally swallow a fly on the walk home you've thrown off your calorie count for the entire month. My view is: eat what you want as long as you don't die. For example, you want to eat a banana? Do it. You want to eat 487 bananas? Don't do it because that will actually kill you. What has led me to this view is the number of times I have been trapped in my bed, held hostage by my own duvet and crippling sense of self-imposed inadequacy, my diet consisting purely of scavenged crisps and whatever brown alcohol lurked at the bottom of a nearby bottle. Much like how great artists have their blue phases, or their bridge phase (I don't know much about art), this diet led me to my 'gout phase'. Being twenty-two and giving yourself gout through poor life choices is less than ideal and, take it from me, not conducive to a functioning mind. Drink plenty of water, eat fruit, eat a green thing (except kale, kale is just lettuce that has stopped trying) and then eat what you bloody want to, you earned it, you ate a green thing. As the saying goes, 'An apple a day keeps the doctor away, an orange a day keeps the postman away, basically if you throw food hard enough people run away.'

Cooking is also a good habit to get into. Microwaveable meals are convenient, but often taste like someone liquidised an old tarp and then covered it in beans. Make yourself a meal from scratch at least once a week and not only will you know you're getting something decent, but it'll give you a sense of accomplishment, a goal that has been achieved. It doesn't need to be anything over the top, you don't need to prepare yourself a gourmet pulled pork salad with diamond dressing and caviar wine, just throw together a curry, make the kitchen messy, enjoy yourself.

When it comes to food another thing we anxious people often ignore is our need to try new things. The anxious mind can easily fall into patterns, you'll find yourself wanting the safe and the familiar, not wanting to go out of your comfort zones, but fuck it, you'll more than likely find something new to become obsessed over. If I hadn't been pushed to try new foods I would still be living on Marmite sandwiches and Birds Eye potato waffles. But now I eat so much more, I also know I hate things too. For instance, and this is where I lose a large portion of you reading this book . . . I hate cheese. Cheese is just milk that's been fucked with and now it's awful. Actually I don't like milk either, it makes me feel sick. (And it was then, reader, that the author realised he might be allergic to dairy.) I also hate tomato ketchup – it's the liquid version of shame, it tastes like grit and makes all food worse, no YOU'RE overreacting. The great thing about trying new things is that you expand your limits a little bit every time, but I'm not going to lie, my favourite meals are still Marmite sandwiches and Birds Eye potato waffles, I mean, they really *are* waffley versatile.*

2. Holidays

An expensive option but one that will usually do the trick is getting the fuck away. To be honest, going on holiday can be very laborious for the anxiously inclined. New places, strangers everywhere, flights, airports (UGH), packing, new languages, new foods and drinks: it is a complete upheaval of our comfort zones. But if you want an escape from reality, to put your worries in a tiny box and throw that box into a lake and then blow up the lake (once again this metaphor has got away from me) and ignore them for a week or a long weekend, then take yourself off somewhere new. Afraid of flying? TRAINS. Afraid of trains? COACH. Afraid of coaches? Probably sensible because being on a coach for a long time is horrendous. Ever tried to use a bathroom on a coach? It's like trying to pour a drink while being beaten up.

However, some of the best therapy you can get is taking every part of your worrisome life and putting it on hold. Yes, it's temporary, but imagine a week without

---

* The recipe for the perfect waffle sandwich. 1. Take two slices of good white bread. 2. Cover bread in Marmite. 3. Put waffle (Birds Eye is recommended but supermarket own brand is fine) in oven for 20 minutes at 200 degrees C. 4. After 20 minutes remove waffle. 5. Put waffle in middle of bread. 6. Holy shit it's brilliant.

checking your emails, or checking Facebook, or even checking the news. Drowning yourself in foreign food and alcoholic beverages you couldn't even try to pronounce even if you'd had seventeen of them. Self-care is treating yourself, telling your body and your brain: 'We are taking a fucking break and you are going to SHUT UP AND ENJOY IT.' A 'getting away from it all' break can be going halfway around the world or it can just be going somewhere that isn't your home for a night. This is one of those times when you can test your own limits, try something new, live life a little – a third motivational quote that should live on a Facebook post.

'We don't deserve a break, breaks are for people who achieve things, people with money, people with real responsibilities.'
'But I am so tired . . .'
'GOOD.'
'Please?'
'Maybe next year, maybe if you've actually done something with your life.'

Of course your own brain is going to try to convince you that you don't deserve a break; this is your brain we are talking about, the same brain that tries to trip you up at every possible turn. But your brain also needs to buffer, it needs a reset, and that can be on a beach, or with a long weekend away to another town; basically somewhere you don't associate with responsibility and worry. You will worry while you are there, but it's about limiting that – there should be no pressure to do things on your downtime. Not many people know this but you are allowed to go to Paris and not visit the Eiffel Tower if you don't want to. Instead you can find a nice coffee shop to relax in. You can go to New York and avoid Times Square if you'd much rather just wander around and try to overhear someone shouting, 'Hey, I'm WALKING HERE!' What do you want to do? What do you want to see? What image have you seen online, from a Pinterest board or an Instagram post, that you want to experience in real life? Do it. You've only got a small window of existing on this planet (didn't mean to cause an existential crisis there by the way), so use it.

3. Animals (Or just finding a dog and staring at it)

Our last stop on this little tour of reward is the fasci-nating world of animals. I am a dog person. Dogs are pure and kind and only ever want to be your friend and maybe help you solve crimes. But some people are cat people, some people are snail people, some people farm ostriches – once again we discover that humans are a diverse bunch of weirdos. Hanging out with animals is proven to make all the happy chemicals in your brain go bonkers, because animals are happy and innocent and everything human beings are not. Except crabs, crabs are inherently evil. Have you ever been chased by a crab? Exactly. If you are like me, and can't get a pet because your landlord is Satan, there are charities that can help, although your anxiety has to be life-altering to qualify, and this still might not get you around the landlord issue. If you need a furry friend to chill out with for a bit, you can always try apps that offer pet-sitting or similar services, or start volunteering at animal shelters, or ask a friend if you can just hang out with their pet for a bit. You're not being rude, but you will ignore all humans and simply follow the animal around the house.

My preferred method of calming down is to just go for a walk and, in a way that is as creepy as humanly possible, stare at other people's dogs and under my breath say: 'Now look at that dog.' I doubt there are many doctors out there who would say, 'Yes, actually stalking strangers' dogs is a perfectly healthy recovery mechanism', and this is why I am better than a doctor. Another animal-related anxiety-helper can be as simple as going to your local farm park. Farm parks are awesome because they aren't zoos and the animals look like they're having a decent time and not trapped in some form of human-orchestrated gibbon prison. At most farm parks you can stroke the animals or, as in my case, get chased by a goose.* Even staring mindlessly at images of animals on the Internet can cause your happy chemicals to spill into your brain, why do you think human beings are so obsessed with cat videos on

---

* Things I have been chased by in this chapter alone: a crab and a goose. At different times by the way. They weren't in cahoots. OR WERE THEY? Maybe there's an international animal conspiracy . . . have I mentioned paranoia in this book yet?

YouTube? It's just another form of escapism, and watching cats get stuck in things is fucking hilarious.

THE REQUIRED METHOD

The previous suggestions are just that, suggestions, but I think the next three things are completely necessary to your recovery, to your life of living with anxiety. They may seem simplistic, but you'd be surprised at how often we don't treat ourselves to the luxury things that other human beings do with great ease, things like a bit of confidence or even just the everyday act of breathing.

1. Positive Thinking

One of our tiny battles with anxiety is starting to not think of yourself as a failure. To not dismiss yourself in every way, shape or form. Confidence is not just for bankers who smoke big cigars and drive cars that act as a phallic replacement service; it's not just for those men who shout 'WAHEY!' in pubs and give each other dead arms. Confidence is something we can all obtain, and something we all deserve. It's the difference between thinking, 'Well today wasn't awful but I could have been better' and 'Today was OK, I did OK, I am getting there.' It's all down to positive thinking. Let's get something straight here, when I refer to positive thinking I am not referring to the concept that has been channelled into a multimillion-pound industry. The idea of 'positive thinking' came from the 1937 book *Think and Grow*

Rich, and since then has been associated with a genre of literature that will try to convince you that thinking in a certain way will lead to your life improving exponentially, that a positive outlook on life will pave the way for your inevitable riches, a yacht, a wife with breasts the size of small moons or a husband who looks like James Bond but if James Bond wasn't a fifty-year-old man, and a house that looks like it came from the mind of a Mexican drug dealer. Thinking 'I deserve a cheesecake', while probably true (you *do* deserve a cheesecake because you are a pretty magnificent human being), won't magically make a cheesecake appear in front of you.

The concept of that sort of positive thinking seems to be a by-product of success, not a path to success itself, so when I talk about positive thinking, I am talking about just not being so fucking hard on yourself all the time. You are no doubt your own worst critic, your own worst enemy, and without justification for being either of these things. It can be easier to be negative about yourself than go through the struggle of positivity, but this is the irrational side of your brain fighting the rational side of your brain again. The irrational telling you that you are literally the worst person on earth, and the rational trying to talk over his shoulder and say 'Well that can't be true at all because Piers Morgan still exists.' If you can actively try to ignore the nasty little voices in your head and look at yourself the way a dog would look at you if you were holding a treat, then you're on the right track.

2. Breathing

If there is one thing in life we should be able to do without any real focus or concentration it's breathing. In . . . out . . . repeat until death. But when you're in the midst of a panic attack, this basic task that we've been doing since birth with little to no effort suddenly becomes as difficult as trying to defuse a bomb while wearing boxing gloves and a blindfold, oh, and the only tool you've been given is a sausage. As your body betrays you and you panic, your body floods with adrenaline and cortisol and your lungs start to emulate those of an asthmatic heron after finishing a 10K. Your body is trying so hard to push blood to the extremities and organs needed for fight or flight that you leave yourself in a state of pure meltdown.

There are three types of stupid breathing you do when you're having a panic attack or just basically being an idiot with your lungs. Shallow breathing, when you're breathing too quickly because your body is stupid. Monitored breathing, when you're thinking about your breathing too much and getting yourself into a tizz about it because your brain is a moron. And over-breathing, when you're shoving too much air into yourself because your body is a dickhead.

There are many breathing exercises you can learn to combat stress and panic, and as you are trying to fill your arsenal with ways to beat anxiety, learning some off by heart can be invaluable. Practise and practise over and over again while you are in a state of calm, so that when you panic you can immediately grab your weapon of choice. The NHS* recommends the following exercise: you can do this sat down, lying down or stood up – dealer's choice. Take a deep breath and let it flow right down into your belly. Get as comfortable as you can, don't start inflating yourself like a balloon. Breathe in through your nose and out through your mouth. Breathe in and count to five. On five, breathe out through your mouth for five. Without a break, go again. Do this for a few minutes. TA-DA! You're now a breathing genius! Put it on your CV immediately.

I use this technique if I am stood on a packed train and I can feel my body tensing up. I start doing this and, nine times out of ten, it stops the oncoming panic before it gets a chance to get going. If you feel like this technique doesn't work for you, ask your therapist, ask a doctor, or have a browse online and find the exercise that puts your lungs back in line. It's all about retraining your lungs to work normally, which sounds ridiculous, but when your body is working against you, you may need to show it who's boss.

3. Anchoring

Now, this technique sounds ridiculous, but hey, we are this far into this book and you haven't complained

---

* Quick note, the NHS website is amazing for finding out more about anxiety and the NHS in general is fucking brilliant, fuck the Tories and their funding cuts. (Sorry, lefty rant over.)

yet. (Have you? Have you been complaining the whole way through? You bastard, behind my back, right in front of my face!) Anchoring is simple: you anchor yourself to the ground. I have found this to be incredibly useful as I am one for feeling dizzy, despondent and generally not in control of the situation, because when the panic comes it can feel like the gravity has been sucked out of the room. All you have to do here is focus all your energy in your body downwards. You lock your knees, tense your leg muscles and anchor yourself in place, then breathe, in and out, simply and normally, with the knowledge that you are anchored in one place. You have now brought an element of control to an event you felt like you did not control. Just breathe.

When you are a fully grown adult, busy adulting around the place, it can feel extremely patronising to have someone teach you how to breathe again, but we need to remember that being an adult is hard, and we often let the simple things crumble beneath us as we put more and more pressure on ourselves. We are too tired to eat so we microwave some garbage. We are too busy to wash properly so we just go to work that day in some sort of hideous state, we are too panicked so we forget to breathe. If there is one thing we deserve, it's to make our lungs obey us again.

'Why don't you just relax a bit?'
'WHY DON'T YOU??'

'I mean, can't you just calm down?'

'CALM? CALM! I AM CALM. THIS IS ME CALM. THE
WEIGHT OF MY LIFE IS CRUSHING ME AND MY BRAIN
IS CONSTANTLY TELLING ME THAT EVERYTHING I DO
WILL NEVER BE ENOUGH AND I DON'T LIKE
MOOMINS AND I THINK THE LADY WHO LIVES
UPSTAIRS IS A SERIAL KILLER I AM SO CALM IT
HURTS.'

'And people say I'm weird.'

Of course everything in this section is subjective, these
are just little prods. You'll probably find your own way
of finding your centre, or your chi – it's whatever you
find healthy and peaceful. And if it involves dogs, please
invite me. We don't have to talk to each other, I promise.

12.
RECOVERY

(AKA The Borrowers, Tony Soprano and Zorbing)

Congratulations! You've survived the day! Now comes the next bit, the whole living your life thing. Now we know how to get from day to day we can focus on the future, and using a little bit of bravery and acceptance, we can make the days better, each day improving upon the last. The goal being to not live underneath the pressure of our anxiety, but to live with our anxiety. The thing about being brave, though, is sometimes it's time to bring in the professionals.

DISCLAIMER: This next section is going to sound a lot like a self-help book, but . . . oh shit I've just written a self-help book haven't I? Oh God I am so sorry.

'Let's go to the doctor's.'
'Why?'

'We need help.'

'Well obviously, but they'll think we're talking shite or being overly dramatic . . .'

'They won't.'

'They'll laugh at us.'

'They won't.'

'But what if—'

'What if what?'

'Exactly.'

'You're probably right.'

'I am always right.'

'Wait.'

'What do you mean wait?'

'Fuck you.'

'What?!'

'You heard, we need this, we deserve this, we are allowed to get better, to get help, I'm not listening to you on this one, you . . . dickhead.'

'Of all the insults you could have used you picked the most mediocre one you could think of? Also, you know I'm not real right? I'm a concept you invented to make you feel less like a freak.'

'Good point, but we're going to the fucking doctor's.'

Let's be clear here: you have admitted you need help and that was the most difficult part. After that it's a breeze. (It is not a breeze, that was just an expression. It's still pretty shit, but now you have a team helping you, like the Power Rangers of anxiety, or the Teenage

Mutant Nervous Turtles.)* The first conversation I had with my GP I was unsure of what to say, what to do, I rambled, my leg shook up and down furiously, I cracked my knuckles and I babbled every uncomfortable symptom out of my face into his. Everything just poured out at once, every niggling little issue I had with the world spilled out of my mouth like a cake out of a hot air balloon (the metaphors are getting weirder).

Finding a doctor can be like finding a partner: some listen intently to every syllable that makes its way past your lips, others just keep saying 'yep' while they keep one eye on the football in the corner. If you are unhappy with your doctor, or if you feel as if they are not listening to you, you can ask to talk to a new one. It's not like dating where there's a long break-up process; it's very unlikely your doctor will turn up outside your window at 3 a.m., holding aloft a boombox playing Peter Gabriel's 'In Your Eyes'. Your doctor is more than likely going to recommend a few different options to you: medication, Cognitive Behavioural Therapy, exposure therapy or a change in lifestyle.

1. Medication

Most people go for door number one. Before taking any form of medication, please have a good look at the side effects that it can cause. Yes, the doctor is the expert but you are an intelligent person who can also have an opinion on the drugs you are putting in your

---

* I really need to start copyrighting these TV show ideas . . .

body, so take an active role and be prepared. Different meds work differently for different people, our brain chemistries all vary slightly, but make sure you are comfortable with the side effects that may occur. Side effects often include: insomnia (goddammit) or sleeping too much (OK, fine), nausea (fun), irritability (no you fuck off), heightened anxiety (perfect), lack of appetite (food is for losers anyway), increased appetite (how many cakes is too many cakes?), fatigue (bags under eyes are model's own) and depressive episodes (woop!). There are various types of anti-anxiety meds out there, from SSRIs (selective serotonin re-uptake inhibitors), which help create more happy serotonin and limit its reabsorption into your noggin (Citalopram and Fluoxetine are types of SSRIs), and SNRIs (serotonin–norepinephrine re-uptake inhibitors), which do the same thing but with serotonin and norepinephrine (another chemical that gets your body ready for fight or flight), to benzodiazepines, which are the Valiums and Libriums of the world – tranquillisers that help keep you calm and relaxed.

Whatever you take, read the label, administer properly and give yourself some time to readjust. Starting a new round of medication will usually leave you with two weeks of feeling like hell while your brain adjusts to a new chemical balance. The two weeks I began taking Citalopram (which I still take today), my mind felt like a game of Tetris where none of the shapes were fitting together. I was constantly tired, I could barely eat anything, I looked like a scarecrow that had originally been deli meat and barber shop hair. However, I've also spoken to people who had very few to no side effects with any of their medications. Just keep these things in the back of your mind as you take this step, that's all.

2. Therapy

Therapy is like talking to a friend but your friend likes talking a lot more than you do and for some reason you're paying for their time and you just want to go home. Before I was told to speak to a therapist I honestly thought therapy was for rich women and Tony Soprano. I know that's a terrible stereotype to have, but that's what I had learned about therapy from watching TV, the main source of my education for all things. I mean, the entire premise of *The Sopranos* is that it's a Mafia dude going to see a therapist (for panic attacks too, nice little tie-in there) and that this isn't what manly men do. The entire show was based on the weird juxtaposition of taking a tough man and putting him in a situation where he couldn't be tough.

I just thought therapy was for overly emotional people, for people who had hidden traumas or had voluntarily seen Gary Barlow live or something. I may have been a tad off on this one, but this is a valuable part of growing up, looking back on your past self and thinking, 'Fucking hell you were a prick', which incidentally is my analysis of 90% of my past. For this section we are going to stick to two different types of therapy that you may be offered: Cognitive Behavioural

Therapy (CBT) and exposure therapy (this one doesn't have an acronym because the acronym ET is already affiliated with a small guy who hangs out with kids and has tiny legs . . . that film sounds weird when you put it like that).

CBT is based on the totally out-there idea that the way we think about situations directly affects how we approach them in real life. It makes sense: if you go to a party and you've been thinking for three days beforehand that it's going to be shit, then you're probably going to have a bad time when you get there because you have convinced yourself of it. If you have never been on a rollercoaster, but have watched seventeen hours of videos of rollercoaster explosions, you probably won't be that keen on going on a rollercoaster.

CBT is brain training – it's taking the tangled-up headphone cables you call a brain and straightening them out to get them working as well as they can again. It is not a practice for stubborn people, as I found out almost immediately when my therapist pretty much told me the way I was thinking about everything was stupid and I should stop it immediately, if not before. CBT is a person who thinks rationally, teaching you, a person who is not rational, to be rational. It is actually pretty simplistic, but it is all the things that your anxious brain has not let you think about or even contemplate. It might be things that your friends and family have told you before, and that you ignored as you thought they were just trying to make you feel better, but the moment a trained professional tells you the same thing, it can feel like you're having an epiphany.

I know how it scary it can feel to begin. Years ago I was sat in the therapist's office, waiting for my first hour of CBT to start, my knee shaking the way it always does when I'm nervous. It was my first session with a new therapist, so I was justifiably nervous. I felt the same way you'd feel on a blind date. 'What if they don't like me? What if they think I'm *too* weird? What if they have one weirdly massive tooth and I just stare at that the entire time?' The therapist came in and introduced himself; he seemed nice, *too* nice – he was obviously up to something. He wanted to prove that I was crazy; one of my enemies must have made sure that he was in the room to certify me as a bonkers headcase, he'd been paid off, he was working against me, I was sure of it. He introduced himself and asked how I was feeling. I replied with: 'Alone, constantly afraid, my eye twitches a lot because I am unsure of things, I worry about everything, also I'm a little chilly.' He looked utterly perplexed and then slid a plastic cup of water over the desk to me.

He then handed me the crazy person form: the form that analyses your mood; every session you fill out this form again so that your therapist can chart your progress. It starts with simple questions like 'Do social situations make you uncomfortable?' and you give a mark out of five (one for HELL NO and five for SHIT YES), but they escalate to 'How often have you had thoughts about harming yourself, please mark out of five' – once again, one means no I haven't thought of this and five means I may be in trouble. I scored highly in this too. I did not want to score highly in this, I even marked myself down a few notches against my better judgement to seem not as crazy as I actually was, but I still came out in the highest percentile (once again, the only test I have ever done well in). The moment you start filling in little squares that quantify your mind, you finally realise that you are not OK, that this isn't fine. CBT is about questioning your brain – it's basically like treating your brain as if it were a petulant child: ignorant, arrogant, stroppy, unwilling to learn.

Over the next six weeks we discussed my work, my lifestyle, my personal life, the universe and everything. I was set homework, I was set challenges, I was set personal goals, all of which either worked or shed light on a problem inside myself that needed solving. I feared speaking to anyone, so I practised with my wife – just talking, that was it, but it helped. I worried everyone saw me as pathetic, so I stopped apologising about everything I would ever do, I tried faux confidence, and it helped. I hated myself, so I gave myself a tiny bit of a break, I argued with my first reactions to any situation, and it helped.

If CBT is the friend who tries to talk you through your problems then exposure therapy is the guy who just punches you straight in the face. Exposure therapy is simple. You don't like crowded spaces? We are going to put you into a crowded space. You don't like deadlines? We are going to make you do every aspect of your life with a deadline. The theory behind this is that putting yourself into these situations will trigger a panic response, and the first time this happens you won't be able to stop it, and it will be horrible, but if you do it over and over again you can start to identify the triggers, you can pre-empt panic attacks and, after enough time, learn to deal with these situations that previously brought you nothing but fear. The chemical reaction of panic does have a time limit, so if you are in a situation that you would normally avoid for long enough, and nothing bad occurs, the panic expires and you learn, consciously and subconsciously, that these events can be overcome.

When I tried this it was with rush hour trains. My therapist recommended that instead of walking (which I had taken to, making my commute infinitely longer but under my control) I take the train as much as I could. He wanted me to see how I dealt with throwing myself into a situation that I hated. I took the tube so much that week that I should have been given a 'most valuable customer' certificate. I had panic attack after panic attack, I jumped off trains between stations and sank into the corners of the platform trying to get my breath back. It was embarrassing and it was horrible and the most annoying thing was that it started to work.

One morning, as my train stopped at Canary Wharf, the stop where everyone in the world pours into the train, I thought to myself 'This is when I am going to panic': the crush of people, the rucksack in the face and accidental punch in the groin, this was about to happen. But predicting it meant I could control it. Anxiety didn't have the jump on me as it used to, I was a step ahead of it for the first time in years. I was starting to control my own reactions. Therapy is a terrifying notion and you may find yourself fighting against it with every fibre of your being. You may think it makes you look weak but that couldn't be further from the truth. Instead of ignoring a problem, or hoping it will simply go away, you are actively choosing to improve yourself, to make yourself better for you, your family and your friends. It's a selfless act.

The first therapist you find may not be for you. As with doctors and dating, you may need some time to find the right one – after all, you don't have to marry the first person you ever dated. Don't let a bad therapist discourage you; there are thousands out there, some recommended by the NHS, some private, some who do online sessions. Stick with it; it can feel like you are working towards a better you, though I'm not going to lie, sometimes buying a fully functional *Star Wars* stormtrooper outfit can do the exact same thing.*

Recovery is a loose term that covers anything that helps to make you feel human again. It's not just the therapy and the meds, it's a lovely bit of everything. There will be moments when you can't see a positive ending in sight, and there may be moments when you can't

---

* It can't do the same thing, therapy is a very serious thing.

possibly imagine anything except the anxious hole in which your mind has buried you. Recovery takes many shapes and forms, but every little victory you encounter helps to reset your brain. A large part of your recovery will be analysing negative patterns in your own life, and having to actively engage in changing yourself. Having to take a long hard look at your entire life can be a less than enjoyable activity, but we want to get better, the path there isn't always pretty.

Often the best things in life, all the things that make us feel comfortable or safe in the moment, are really, truly bad for us. That's how much the human existence makes sense. Self-destruction isn't just about going on a three-week bender and waking up in Croydon with the name 'Becky' tattooed on your inner thigh. Self-destruction is any activity we partake in that is in some way detrimental to our lifestyle. It's also difficult to generally define self-destructive tendencies, as they are, like our anxiety, unique to each person. Not leaving the house is self-destructive, as you're damaging your own psyche while convincing yourself that you are protecting yourself. Drinking too much coffee on a day-to-day basis is self-destructive as you are purpose-fully feeding your anxiety. Smoking, drinking, overindulgence in anything can be self-destructive.

Self-destruction, in this case, is a kind of avoidance behaviour. Think objectively for a second about what activities or daily ventures you indulge in that could be seen as avoidance behaviours. What you are avoiding may not even be something physical, or something in your day-to-day; it can be a simple avoidance of reality. However, the difference between escapism, which is a vital part of our lives and enables us to gain some rationality in this world, and avoidance, which is an active evasion of responsibility, self-care or healthy (physical and emotional) living, is huge. Not to contradict myself entirely (fuck it I am going to do it anyway), but I am not going to tell you that any avoidance behaviours you find yourself indulging in need to be stopped immediately. In my experience, these behaviours are in place to help us, to give us a nod in the direction of what needs to change, a clue to whatever may be causing these behaviours in the first place. But basically I'm saying you need to figure out – 'What am I running from?' Just to go for the full cliché here, I was running away from any responsibility, any sense of self and any idea of reality, so I partook in avoidance behaviours that helped me feel like these things weren't important.

Have you ever taken stock of your own life in serious detail while trying to be proactive about it? It's awful. I said two paragraphs ago that it was going to be less than enjoyable and I would just like to reiterate that here. Our clichéd idea of self-realisation usually involves someone going on a spiritual tour in a far-away country, sitting cross-legged on beaches while wearing an array of beads and silks, and appropriating someone else's culture for a bit to steal the best bits they can remember, then coming back home and not shutting the fuck up about Bali or some shit for seven years. But self-realisation is actually just thinking to yourself 'Oh fuck' when examining your own life. That's it. The 'oh fuck' moment (or as Oprah calls it the 'ah ha' moment, but I prefer mine) can come from a hangover one morning, or a misinterpreted interaction with another human being. It can be a small thing or a life-altering event, but it is a catalyst to finding your own path to recovery.

Accepting that we have negative aspects of our own personalities can be incredibly difficult because we don't want to admit that we have flaws or foibles – the 'ignorance is bliss' strategy works so much better here, but to reprogramme our minds we need to find the issue causing the problem. A way of thinking about this is: are you trying to do what other people expect of you, or are you trying to be happy? Competitive comparability (the idea of comparing your life to everyone else's) and self-inflicted sociological expecta-tions (your own plan for your life that you have in your head that you're not currently keeping up with) can be the fuel for the anxiety fire, and if we are living in a mindset where we are trying to *do* instead of simply *be*, we will constantly feel as if we are failing. Are you doing what you are doing because you think it's what others want of you, what others expect of you, or are you doing what you are doing because you want to be happy? It should always be the latter. Anxiety is a selfish disorder and sometimes the only way to fight it is by being selfish. Think about what you need, what you want and what you want your life to be.

The bright side is that not everything has to be about

changing your life or altering your way of being and striving towards a better you. One of the healthiest things you can ever do is to take stock of your life, accept that you have some issues, that you may have some self-destructive tendencies and think, 'Yeah but I am still fucking awesome.' With whatever shit you've got going on in your life, you can always remember that you are being the best version of yourself that you can be at this point. This doesn't have to be external confidence (the confidence that we all wish we had and desperately try to convey); this is about inner confidence, confidence that is just for you. It's a gift you can keep secret and you can keep away from everyone else in the world – this is just you feeling good about being you. It's not ego, it's not self-importance, it's self-belief. The idea that you can finally look at a version of yourself that you are proud to have created. You may still be nervous, you still may be scared and filled with irrational worry and fear, but you are surviving with all these things stacked against you, you will fight tiny battle after tiny battle and come out on top, stronger and more experienced than before. This is not a faux speech (though if you did want to read it like Bill Pullman in *Independence Day* that would be awesome, thank you), this is just me being honest with you and about what you can achieve with your place in this confusing and terrifying world.

Recovery starts with acceptance, recovery continues with help, and a big part of getting help is talking to others about your own emotions. At this stage you are probably pretty good at denying your emotions, keeping them stored deep, deep down where no one could ever find them. To confront them and to be honest about them is something your brain has been convincing you not to do for such a long time that you are no longer sure if you can do it or not. There's a big difference between a drunken Twitter rant at 3 a.m. and actually being honest and pouring your heart out to another human being. The latter is a lot healthier.

Now the way this works is completely up to you. Because your anxiety is unique to you, your recovery will also be individual. You might run straight to a doctor and ask for help, or you might want to talk to someone close to you first. After spending so much time going through this in your own head, the first time you vocalise your issues might be confusing, but you might also come to some conclusions all on your own thanks to a simple conversation. For example, one of the first conversations I had about my anxiety was with a friend, and I said: 'Every negative thing that happens around me is my fault.' They replied: 'Why do you think that?' Well, fuck, when I had told myself that statement over and over again at no point did I ask *why*. Of course when I thought about it there was no why, but I felt like a fucking idiot, because I had never come to that realisation by myself. It's the equivalent of when you're in an argument with a partner, and they say: 'Well, give me an example of a time I did that' and your mind goes blank. You're sure you have a retort somewhere, but it's fallen out of your head like a cake from a hot air balloon (that's still not working as a metaphor, is it?).

Opening up to a family member or a partner or a friend can be a testing experience; you are baring your soul to someone who holds certain expectations of you. Human beings don't like showing vulnerability: we are born, we persevere and we die – that's our lot in life. In the middle bit we try not to cause too much of a fuss – and when we open up to people, we do feel like we're causing a fuss. This may be more of a British thing, like how even though we are the nation who invented queuing most of us still wouldn't say anything if someone cut in front of us. Oh, in our heads they would be getting the bollocking of a lifetime, but in the real world, they get a tut and a stink-eye. It is the British way. If you are not comfortable talking to your family, ask a friend; if you are not comfortable talking to a friend, try a therapist or one of the online talking services the NHS provides. All are healthy ways of vocalising your internal battles. If you don't think your friends or family will understand, be honest with them: just tell them that you need their help. If they ask you what anxiety is, simply reply that it's a part of you, it's worry on overdrive, and if they still don't understand ask if they wouldn't mind reading about it. This is you creating your support network; you're allowed to ask for favours, you're allowed to ask for a hand to hold or a shoulder to cry on.

BECOMING YOU AGAIN

You are not striving to be 'normal'. Normal involves going to garden centres, reading the *Telegraph* and making your own jam. Normal people are terrifying, they like the music of Sting unapologetically, they have caravanned, their favourite colour is beige. You are extraordinary. Yeah, you may not leave the house and maybe you're scared of passing your driving test because being in charge of an automobile seems like too much responsibility for you, but you are extraordinary. Anxiety recovery is 80% hard work and 20% self-confidence. Remember self-confidence? It was that thing you used to have before terror became the all-important part of your life. If Donald Trump can look in the mirror in the morning and think he's brilliant then you definitely can: you are nowhere near as bad a human being as Donald Trump. You could drive a bus through a nun convention and you still wouldn't be as much of a dick as old DT.

In your head you'll have an ideal version of yourself. You are probably glorious-looking, with a full head of hair, wonderfully flawless skin, massive genitals (not sure if that is a thing women wish for but let's skip over that quickly), riches, friends, a sense of humour that would make Robin Williams asthmatic and the raw charm of a sexy Italian barman with a degree in charm from Charm University.* The reality can be quite

---

* If you read that and thought 'Oooh, a *Blackadder* reference' then you're a very good person.

different; you are after all only human, susceptible to human faults and human idiosyncrasies, so you can never expect yourself to be anything more than human.

Humans fall into two categories: there are bad humans and good humans. Bad humans listen to music out loud off their phones on public transport and buy the *Sun*. Good humans worry about other humans, they give to a charity, ask if a co-worker is OK, offer to buy a drink for a friend if they know that friend is a little broke. Try to be a good human; that is all you can expect of yourself. Be a good human, take the experiences and the fear you have had to endure and use them as a strength. Shit can always get worse, as various biblical proverbs would have said if they weren't censored by prudes in robes, but with anxiety, with mental health disorders, your brain has shown you at your worst, you have dealt with pain and loneliness, what else can hurt you? A tiger attack? (Yes, that would definitely hurt actually.)

What do you do after your anxiety has calmed down? You've spent so much of your life terrified of the outside world, of your own mind, of every foreseeable consequence you could invent for yourself, so what's next? The next bit is pretty OK actually. Recently, I sat in a bar in central London with a group of friends. I had gone through the usual phases of the build-up to going out. What excuses could I use to get out of this? Which excuses hadn't I used before so it would still seem genuine? Then I got past that. I realised I had to go

– not for them, they were in a group so if I wasn't there they would have a good time regardless. I needed to go for me. For the first time in six years, I was putting myself first. Of course the safe option was to stay at home, binge watch *The X-Files* and strap on some kind of crisp nosebag, as I had been doing every night for the better part of a year, but I had a chance to change and I took it, because fuck anxiety. My hand tightened around the tube pole as my train approached the station, with every second I was getting closer to becoming a better person, and it was fucking terrifying. The obvious thoughts ran through my head. What if they all think I'm boring? What if I am so anxious the entire time that I make it seem like I don't want to be there? What if I offend anyone? What if I start talking and I see everyone's eyes slowly dying in their faces? I was sweating through my shirt already, but a-HA! I had packed deodorant, like someone who was prepared for things would do. Quick sidenote, if you apply deodorant to your armpits while stood on a corner in central London, a lot of Chinese tourists will think that you've started a performance piece.

The fact that my big anxiety breakthrough story is simply 'going to a bar with some people I know' tells you a lot about the nature of the condition. The irrationality, how it affects every tiny little thing you do, the absolute absurdity of it. I knew how ridiculous I was being as I stood outside the venue and chain-smoked, psyching myself up for what was essentially just a nice night out. Anxiety doesn't do perspective, you know at any point that people have things worse than you, that this isn't the worst thing to happen to someone in the history of everything ever, but to you it feels like that. To you, every anxious moment feels like the end of the world. I put out my last cigarette on a bin and straightened my shirt. I could hear the rational and irrational parts of my brain arguing over and over.

'We should leave.'
'No, let's go in.'
'If we leave now we haven't fucked this up.'
'We won't know if we fuck this up until we go in.'

I went with the 'fuck it, why not?' option, which is one of my favourite options for anything nowadays. What is the worst that can happen? I embarrass myself? That's just part of my personality, I can deal with that! People think I am boring? Well that's their problem, I am fucking interesting, I know the Marvel Cinematic universe inside and out, and that's a talent – I could put that on my CV; actually I know a lot of random trivia after nights spent awake in Wikipedia holes, so if anything goes wrong, I can use that. After a wobbly introduction, and a catastrophic prediction of how the night should have gone, it went fine. It was a nice night between friends. I didn't speak much but I chose my words carefully and they landed well in the conversation, it was my first big step on the way back to becoming who I was, who I thought I could be. I had achieved something I had once considered utterly terrifying. I walked out of the bar and thought to myself, next time I'll make it two hours, then the time after that two and a half hours, it's baby steps but that's OK.

Your recovery will be unique to you. Don't forget that. No one understands your mind like you do, and you will know best how to deal with the stupid voices in your head. I don't know you, and I don't pretend to know you. For me I find a quiet drink in an old man's pub a source of relaxation, for you it could be zorbing or bukkake. Your life is your own, your mind is your own and your recovery is your own. If you think you need help, get help. If you think you need a hand, ask for a helping hand. If you need to talk, ask someone to listen. Not to sound like a fucking informercial here, but the only thing stopping you is you, and you can be a bit of a dick at times.

13.

REPRESENTATION AND STIGMA

(AKA Marmite Haters, Frank Bruno and Avatar)

So, you've survived a day in the life of an anxious human being, and you've started to think about how you might even learn to *enjoy* those days. You deserve a good sit-down, a massage, maybe even some bus milk because now you've developed a taste for it and it's all you can think about and the cravings are becoming too much. We all reward ourselves differently. We look after ourselves to the best of our abilities, but unfortunately the tiny battles do not stop there. We've helped ourselves, now it's time to look outwards, to see how we can help others, how we can use any knowledge we have gained on our own to assist our fellow sufferers. We are a community, yes it's a weird community and our meet-ups would probably be very awkward and get cancelled at the last minute, but we are a community. Anxiety never truly goes away, we learn to live with it, to live in spite of it. We have to learn to look after each other, because we know how shit it can be.

How did you know you were anxious? How did you finally come to the conclusion that your mind works differently from other people's? For some the trigger is a trip to the doctor's, where one of the diagnoses is some form of anxiety. But for others it is never addressed, it's just seen as a part of their personality, as much as a bad sense of humour or having the inclination to put milk in the teacup first before the boiling water (I mean come on). They assume, or rather, we assume, that this is our lot in life, that this is our normal. How are we supposed to know better? Without accurate representation and education we are, to put it bluntly, ignorant. And on the other hand, if a condition or a way of being is demonised, or seen as weak, we will never admit to it afflicting us. Human beings are proud, we want to be perceived as tragically mediocre at the very least, or just to project the image that we aren't struggling with everything ever. We compare ourselves to strangers, we look down on ourselves for not achieving standards that we have imposed on ourselves. When asked 'Are you OK?' we are more likely to lie, to say 'Yeah fine', instead of, 'Actually I don't know.' The latter leads to questions and to a further conversation, which we try to avoid unless we are with someone we designate as a healthy influence on our life. So mostly, we lie and keep our problems our own.

Person 1: 'Hello! How are you?'

Person 2: 'Good thanks! You?'

Person 1: 'Oh, well, I'm tired all the time, I mostly spend my time staring blankly at my phone while flicking between the same two apps, my diet consists mostly of whatever brown liquor I can find around the house and crisps that I have scavenged from the crevices of my furniture. My bones hurt and I know it's because I have a bad diet and don't exercise but thinking about changing the fundamental elements of my life terrifies me so I resign myself to a lifetime of repetition and mediocrity until I eventually perish in what I assume will either be an avalanche of my own failures or a sex-related jazz accident.'

Person 2: 'So . . . It's been nice seeing you. I have to go.'

'Honesty is the best policy' – the proverb seen on the inspirational posters lining every kitsch furniture shop – is attributed to Benjamin Franklin, which is slightly ironic as he nicked the idea from Thomas Jefferson, who said, 'Honesty is the first chapter in the book of wisdom.' It is, however, never an idiom I have followed in my own life, mostly because I am a gigantic disaster of a person but also because humanity is more complicated than that. The main idioms I follow in my life are:

⚡ 'You don't truly know yourself until you have spent an entire day in a pub, by yourself, and got really drunk.'

⚡ 'Never microwave a jar of Marmite.'

⚡ 'Every single person you encounter is a potential threat and should be treated as such.'

⚡ 'Just because it's on offer doesn't mean you need to spend the extra 70p for another bottle of orange squash. Three bottles of orange squash is too much orange squash.'

⚡ 'A friend's house is where your phone connects to the wifi automatically.'

⚡ 'Geese are just ducks on bath salts and steroids.'

They make sense to me, but once again, I am a massive disaster man.

The fact is, culturally we Brits are less accustomed to revealing our emotions than our European or American counterparts. Therapy is big business in the US, it has become more normalised than it has over here in ol' Blighty. Still, when a Brit says they are in therapy it brings a lot of questions: 'What's wrong with them?', 'Am I safe to be around them?', 'Can they work?', 'Can they raise a family?' Of course this applies more to mental health in general than it does to anxiety specifically, but the stigma is still there, the lack of knowledge is still prevalent. Problems understanding anxiety seem to be rooted in the idea that 'feeling anxious' and 'suffering with anxiety' are two identical things, when of course we know that they are wildly different. Both of these subjects are rooted in worry, but feeling anxious, as we have said before, is a natural and perfectly normal human reaction. Anxiety is the opposite of this, a genetic cock-up, an irrational human overreaction.

When we start to talk about anxiety, we normalise it. When we discuss mental health problems with a brave face and an informed outlook we can bring the conversation into the public light. Once again, one in four people suffers with a mental health problem in their lifetime. To put this into perspective, only one in three people in the UK likes Marmite, but they are quite happy to say how much they like Marmite in public even though they are in the minority and some may find this a disgusting, if not offensive, practice. But they don't mind talking about it. OK, fine, that may have been a terrible example. Talking about anxiety with your peers can be a liberating experience, talking about anxiety with your therapist or doctor can feel like a life-changing moment, discussing your woes with a partner or a friend can make everything in the world seem that little bit more bearable.

Have you ever been sat in a pub with some friends and a new person, a friend of a friend, joins the group?

You are out of your comfort zone, you don't know this person, this person could be an alien spy for all you know, but you get onto a conversation about a film, and you both love this film, you have a connection, and suddenly you are back in the conversation. One day we will be able to do that with anxiety. We will be open, we will be able to discuss our fears, our foibles and our conditions with the ease of discussing the latest Marvel blockbuster, but until then, we are just trying our best. While terrifying, vocalising your thoughts can bring you a new sense of scale to your own condition, articulating your feelings through purposefully worded heart-to-hearts can help you realise things that your anxiously inclined mind has been hiding from you for quite some time. Remember, your anxiety doesn't want you to get better. *You* want you to get better, so don't let your anxiety dictate your recovery. And we come back to the golden rule of anxiety: don't do anything you don't want to do.

STIGMA AND HOW TO TALK ABOUT ANXIETY

Stigma exists at its most basic level due to lack of knowledge. Stigma is fear, stigma is the association of something with a negative due to an ill-informed conclusion. Fear powers stigma and stigma powers fear, it's one of those wonderfully nonsensical circles in life, like a snake eating itself or an eel eating itself or basically any animal that is mostly neck just eating itself. Can a giraffe eat itself? These are some of the hard-hitting questions we will get to investigate in this chapter.

We've spoken about our worries, about how our brains are going to jump to the stupidest conclusion no matter what we do, so now we introduce a whole new bag of stress. Are you – and by 'you' I mean 'we' – going to be treated negatively for the way our brains are wired? I emphasise that last point, as we cannot help how the tangled heaps of nonsense that are our brains are constructed, and we need to know this to battle our own stigmas around mental health. Mental health problems *are not your fault*, they are not a negative aspect of your being, they are not a statement on who you are or your place in this world, they are simply a part of you. And this part of you can be managed, it can be controlled but it cannot be eradicated to turn you into someone you are not. Living with mental health problems often makes you a stronger person. You've been to places most people have never been, you've analysed your life and deconstructed yourself more than any other person could, and you are stronger for it. If you see four people in the street, four random strangers, the odds are that one of them is battling a mental health disorder, and unless one of them is wearing a huge sign saying 'BANANAS', you won't be able to tell the difference. So why do we live in this culture of stigma? Where tabloid papers rub their hands together gleefully if anyone famous is on any sort of prescription medication for mental health disorders? Where terms like 'mad' or 'crazy' are thrown around as common derogatory terms?*

The word crazy can be found back as far as the 1500s, but then it was spelled 'craze' and simply meant 'unwell'. It was the brilliant minds of the 1600s that took crazy to mean 'someone of unsound mind'. Terms like 'mental', 'bonkers' and 'looney' are found in the English language (in their derogatory forms) from the 1900s, but all have the same connotation: that person, whoever they are, is different and we should therefore fear them. Language changes, the way we use words changes, and as we grow as a society we learn that some words are just a bit offensive† to others. It's not 'PC GONE MAD', it's common sense and compassion. It's also freedom of speech. Yes, of course you are allowed to say words that are seen as uncouth or hurtful, no one is stopping you saying them, but in the same way, no one can stop me calling you a fuckwit for doing it. Freedom of speech is good like that.

You just have to look at some of the headlines in the news over the last two decades to realise the stigma is still prevalent.

---

* I realise the irony of saying that we shouldn't use the word mad while I have been using it a lot in this book. But there is a big difference between using it as an insult or a judgement rather than a self-detrimental safety blanket to mock your own mental health problems.

† If you ever meet me ask me about the time I swore in my wedding speech, it's a good example of how some people find swearing funny, and others really REALLY do not.

In 2003 the English 'newspaper' (newspaper in quotation marks there as it's as much a newspaper as I am a guinea pig) the *Sun* were forced to apologise after an outcry for publishing, on their front page, 'Bonkers Bruno Locked Up', a story about ex-boxer Frank Bruno being hospitalised for depression.

In 2015 the *Daily Mail* ran an article, on their front page again, 'Why On Earth Was He Allowed To Fly?', about the pilot Andreas Lubitz, who suffered from depression and was at the helm when a plane crashed. It transpired that Lubitz did in fact crash the plane on purpose, but this is hardly a symptom of depression, and yet the headline and subsequent story suggested that anyone with a mental health problem shouldn't be allowed certain careers because of their disorder.

In 2013, the *Sun*, again, published a front page that said '1,200 Killed By Mental Patients'. It doesn't matter that the article was later proved to be misinterpreting statistics, because the damage was already done. The retraction never made a front page. These two newspapers are the biggest-selling in Britain and when a young person, or anyone for that matter, who already feels isolated reads these sorts of headlines, they are less likely to want to speak honestly about their own mind, the emotions, the issues and the feelings they deal with on a day-to-day basis, and therefore less likely to get the help they need.

This nonsense doesn't end with the newspapers, it's bloody everywhere. It's in the TV and film industries. It's 'psycho' or 'mental patient' fancy dress costumes at

Halloween. It's Debbie on Facebook who declares 'I'm just a bit mad, me!' You're not 'mad', Debbie, you had a glass of wine at 3 p.m., if anything you're four hours behind the rest of us. The vilification of mental health is so entrenched in western culture that mentally ill people are all seen as bad guys, weirdos, a menace to be avoided at all costs. Nine in ten people with mental health disorders will experience some form of stigma or discrimination in their life.* As Ruby Wax says: 'Why, if any other organ in the body is damaged, do you receive sympathy, but not if the problem is with your brain?' Society, as a collective, tends to associate mental health with criminality. We've all seen the horror movies where the 'escaped mental patient' does a nonsense and goes full flapjack and chases a family through a field or something. One of the best ways of minimising stigma is to reject this harmful narrative. There is a very simple fact that dispels the 'all people with mental health problems are dangerous' rhetoric, and that's that those with mental health problems are much more likely to harm themselves than anyone else.

Is this overcompensation by society because the reality is pretty boring? Being 'mad' is actually just really fucking annoying. We're not the tragic artists, the comic relief, the neighbourhood nut jobs, we are just people. People expect you to lose your mind at any moment, to be overly emotional, to go on a killing rampage with a weaponised hen (I haven't thought about killing rampages

* https://www.time-to-change.org.uk/mental-health-statistics-facts

enough to nail down the details, evidently), when the reality is just lonely confused people who want nothing more than to lie in bed all day and not have any attention drawn to themselves. It's the little things, the whispers in the office once you have told a co-worker about your condition, the fear that the company is planning to get rid of you, sitting in the doctor's office feeling like you are wasting their time because it's just 'all in your head', feeling like you've let your family down and that they will blame themselves for your condition – the guilt that goes hand in hand with anxiety is pretty shit.

And while you are dealing with these internal worries, external threats creep in too. Society still thinks that mothers with mental health conditions aren't as good at parenting as mothers with perfectly chemically balanced brains. (We can't all be neurotypical, Karen.) Some employees would still prefer the 'normal' employee compared to the defective alternative. Even with equality acts in place, these things still happen, and we still read about them, we still think 'What if that were me?' or 'Is that what my boss/friends think about me?' We have discussed in detail how the anxious noggin likes to jump to conclusions, to take the worst-case scenario as a definite and to over-think and over-analyse it at excruciating length, and this happens every time we read a headline, or see a story, or hear someone we thought was a friend use an offensive word. Frankly, having a mental health condition is tiring enough, you already believe that the world is against you, you don't need it reinforced over and over again.

Anxiety is seen by some as a weakness. This may shock you but anxiety is not a weakness. Suffering from anxiety does not mean that you are a failure, it does not mean that you are any less of a human being than any other walking flesh sack on this planet. You cannot define a human being by one unique attribute of their personality. You are not your anxiety, you are you, but you have anxiety.

Here is a handy list of things that are failures:

⚡ The movie *Avatar* (not in box-office terms, obviously, just because it was utterly shit)

⚡ Michael Gove's 2016 prime ministerial election bid

⚡ Chickens (chickens evolved from velociraptors, how can you fail that hard?)

⚡ Donald Trump's wig

⚡ Any film version of any video game

THINGS THAT ARE NOT FAILURES:

⚡You

It's time for another poorly-cobbled-together analogy! Your brain is an engine . . . hang on, it really kind of is! OK this analogy is actually off to a good start. It drives you, it helps you and, if one thing were to break in a car engine, you wouldn't scrap the entire car, you would fix the one thing wrong with the engine. Anxiety is that thing: just because one thing is wrong with your brain, doesn't mean you are wrong – actually most of it is working brilliantly, there's just one little bit that could do with a tune-up. Because anxiety doesn't want you to get better, you spend your entire life in such a dizzying anxious storm that when it comes to the time that you could possibly deal with your anxiety, you're too tired to do it. Good isn't it?

Another annoying aspect about life in general is that you have to put the work in to see effects. I saw it very much like my exercise regime: I was doing no exercise and wasn't getting any thinner. If anything, I was becoming more spherical day by day. It just made no sense! It's the same with anxiety. I wasn't sleeping, but I wasn't drinking any less coffee and I was taking more work on every day; I never made the correlation that the excess worry I was inflicting upon myself was affecting my sleep patterns. I didn't want to leave the house, so I didn't – it was that simple. It took the problem away completely. If there was any sort of crowd around me I could feel a panic attack coming up from inside me like an apocalyptic burp, so I avoided crowds: simple, done. My anxiety had overwhelmed me, it was in control, it was growing like a fungus or a parasite. It had won.

When I was first diagnosed with anxiety, my initial feeling was guilt. The feeling of guilt wasn't intentional,

it appeared randomly, and though it might have had something to do with how little I understood it at the time I felt in my entire being that I had let myself down, that I had disappointed my wife, my family, my friends.*
I was ashamed of myself for being so weak. When I had left the doctor's office several years earlier with my diagnosis of depression I'd felt like I finally had a reason for myself, that I knew why I was in some way different. However, my anxiety diagnosis hit me harder. I had been doing everything I could to be a normal person, to behave like a functioning human being, and I still felt like a complete fuck-up.

The stigma was clearly all there, because everything I knew of anxiety I had learned through books and TV: that the anxious character was usually the first one to go, the panicky one you watched while thinking: 'God I hope they shut up and get eaten in a minute.' I was one of those guys now. How did I become the guy that everyone wanted to get eaten for being too annoying? It's the difference between the guy from *Jurassic Park* who panics and runs to the toilet (possibly running to the toilet to void himself as his body prepares itself for

* It felt like that wonderful joke about the boy made out of balloons who goes to a school made of balloons where all of his friends are also made out of balloons. One morning he goes into school with a needle, and the headmaster calls him into the office and says, 'You've let the school down, you've let your classmates down and most importantly you've let yourself down.' Sorry, I just love that joke.

the fight or flight response, don't tell me this book hasn't helped clear up some film plot points!) and Hudson, Bill Paxton's character from *Aliens*, who has a break-down while fighting an enormous horde of bastards. Which would you rather be? Hudson obviously: he panics but he still gets shit done. The dude on the toilet gets used as an appetiser. I stood at a bus stop, a ciga-rette shaking in my hand as I stuffed the prescription paper in my jacket pocket and began to flick through the leaflets and materials the doctor had given me. I defined myself as this problem now: I wasn't a person who suffered with anxiety, I was an anxious person.

You know when people are about to die and their entire life flashes before their eyes? When I got diag-nosed I did that, but with every social situation I'd ever been in that I had probably ruined with my anxiety. Every conversation I had been quiet in, every time I had probably embarrassed myself with anxious silence. I remembered being sat in a bar with some friends in Soho, peeling a label off my beer bottle as my left leg shook up and down, I must have looked like a demented Weeble. I didn't join in conversations as I was so terri-fied of saying something that the group would interpret as idiotic, so I protected myself with silence. Personally I had had a good night: I got to listen to my friends enjoying themselves, I was there, I laughed at jokes, I tried my best, but it still hadn't felt enough. To me, it felt like I had ruined the evening, like my silence and habitual awkwardness had put a dampener on the night. My mind raced through the previous years of social interactions: How had I embarrassed myself? Had people regretted asking me to come out with them? Every situation that I had invented a problem for had one factor in common: me. I was the problem. I have a problem. I am a problem.

So I did what any sensible adult would do: I became a weird hermit who threw himself into work and ignored everything else. My wife could barely get a conversation out of me. I had convinced myself that she was better off without me, that she could do so much better than this crumbling heap of confusing twat that I had become. I didn't speak to my family so as not to disappoint them (another problem invented solely by me). I rarely talked to my friends, I became distant at work and, because of this, I felt alone.

Eventually, you finally start fighting back. I wasn't sleeping, so I saw the doctor and asked for a short course of sleeping tablets, I cut out the coffee, I cut down on my work. I didn't want to go outside, but I would walk to the shops and back, sometimes to buy bread, often to not buy anything at all, but I was out of the house. I saw the crowds coming and I started doing breathing exercises, I analysed the situation before I was surrounded by it, I had pre-empted my anxiety for once, I got here before it could surprise me. When you are in that anxious moment, when you can feel your heart beating like a heavy-metal drummer's bass drum, and you can feel your chest tightening, you can't escape it – anxiety is there. Anxiety is in control, but if you can get in front of your anxiety, if you can think two steps ahead, like an assassin, an anxious assassin (that's a great idea for a TV show), you can get into the right frame of mind before you are immersed in panic.

And soon I started to realise that if I had taken a moment to truly analyse my life I would have seen that I was far from alone in this: I had a wife who loved me, a family who supported me, friends who asked after me, colleagues who were concerned. My anxiety had convinced me that this was all fake or circumstantial. I looked in the mirror and saw a freak. I had fallen into a very dark place from which I thought there was no escape. I was immersed in the stigma of mental illness and I didn't think anyone on the planet cared. Mental health problems are inherently selfish, I have said this over and over again but they are, they turn your attention inwards and make the outside world seem like a cold dark place that doesn't care.

Stigma is fear: on one hand you have the people who are afraid of people with mental health problems and what they may do to them, and on the other hand you have people with mental health problems who fear how the general public perceive them. It's another anxiety circle. Just like how you worry about a thing, then you worry that you are worrying about the thing and not doing the thing, and that goes in circles and circles until you lose your mind . . . It's the same with stigma. The public are afraid of people with mental health issues, and those with mental health issues are afraid of the public. So the more we talk about it, the stronger we will get, both as a community and a society. And this is where representation comes in.

The way we receive information has changed drastically over the last two decades. I spoke earlier about the idea of catastrophic thinking, but it's important to look at the other side of this idea. Previous generations gained their knowledge of the world from their parents, peers, biased newspapers, while current generations gain knowledge from an endless supply of opinions that can fit into a device no bigger than a deck of cards. Obviously this has positive and negative implications, and I've tried to look at both.

The negatives are the way we receive pieces of bad news in such quick succession that our brains don't get a break, and the trolls and the people who use this new way of getting information to spread fear, hate, bile and terror. But as we get caught up in this tide of information, it's easy to miss the people doing good work amidst it, the people trying to help others. We miss the fact that most people aren't trying to spread messages of fear, but rather messages of hope. When I was growing up I had one understanding of mental illness, and that was that it was solely associated with rock stars killing themselves at the age of twenty-seven. That's it. There weren't any media outlets that I had access to to tell me why my rock heroes were passing at such a young age; the news reporters didn't mention it. When I finally realised I might have my own issues I didn't know what was wrong; it wasn't something I'd ever read about. My knowledge of depression was limited to the lyrics of Nick Drake's later work, my knowledge of anxiety came from quirky characters in sitcoms. There was nothing about these things that brought these ideas into reality for me.

Nowadays you hear about mental health being fashionable, that it's a topic of the month, when in fact what has happened is that people are only now becoming comfortable talking about it in public; and the impact that is having is astonishing. To read an article or to hear an interview with another human being who you can relate to in a way that you have never felt before is an incredible thing. We are at a stage where people are brave enough to discuss these invisible illnesses with each other, to share stories, and while it's very unlikely that another person's experience will be identical to yours, hearing this subject discussed is invaluable. From every celebrity talking openly about a problem, to every blog post from someone you've never heard of, the subject is being normalised. And when you normalise something in this way, you take away the power of the stigma and you start breaking down the barriers. It will of course take time, because everything does. Rome wasn't built in a day – how could it have been? They've been erecting a building opposite my flat for two years and it hasn't changed that much, and if this is how all building works operate I theorise Rome would have taken about 1,200 years to complete. I lost my train of thought there . . .

A LIST OF THINGS YOU LEARN IN SCHOOL:

⚡ The mitochondria is the powerhouse of the cell

⚡ Everest is a very big mountain

⚡ Don't ever have sex because God will chop your dick off

⚡ China's third largest export is furniture

THINGS YOU DON'T LEARN IN SCHOOL:

⚡ How to do taxes

⚡ How to ask your parents for money even though you've just been paid but you spent all your wages on chicken nuggets and a Deadpool costume

⚡ How to deal with any aspect of adulthood in a sensible way

⚡ Anything about mental health disorders at all

The correlation between people being diagnosed and the conversation around mental health increasing isn't a coincidence; it's down to the fact that we can now feel comfortable talking about things that we previously hid out of shame; the fact that with every blog post, every article and every tweet talking about mental health problems, we are helping someone who has struggled and has finally found that someone else is suffering just like them. It is not a trend of mental health problems, it is simply relatability, honesty, compassion flowing through humanity in a way that had before only been reserved for physical diseases, not the invisible ones. The more we recognise mental health problems as something that can happen to anyone and everyone, that they are universal and in every way just as devastating as physical injuries or diseases, the more we take stigma away, the more people we can help.

As we saw in the chapter about the Internet and my interviews with the young people at Off The Record, young people have more understanding of mental health conditions than any generation before them, but this usually isn't through education, more through osmosis or self-research. The actual education system is not equipped to properly teach or deal with young people's mental health issues. So right now it is up to charities, to independent organisations to raise awareness of these problems. This is by no means the fault of the teachers or the schools, it is down to the systems put in place and a simple lack of funding. At the heart of it though, it's up to everyone to help, to spread information, experiences, give advice when you can, to be open-minded and to be compassionate. Anxiety doesn't have a specific set of symptoms like a broken arm does, so it's never clear how to approach the subject, but we can ask ourselves or ask others if they are OK, if they need help, if they need an ear to lean on or a shoulder to talk to. The burden of education rests on the shoulders of all of us. You know, just in case we didn't have enough to fucking worry about.

14.
YOU ARE OK
(AKA You Are OK)

The combination of three little words can have a lot of impact on the human psyche. 'I love you', 'I brought cake', 'Where's my son?', 'Here's fifty quid', 'You are OK'. Three words can change your life. The moment you hear 'You are OK', your life can start getting back to normal. Often these are the words you say to yourself at first. Quietly, if not silently. A little motto of self-confidence, building yourself up to prepare for an event with which you are entirely uncomfortable. Those of us who spend our days consumed by anxiety tell ourselves that we are OK when we step outside the house. We tell ourselves that we are OK the moment we enter a busy space. We tell ourselves that we are OK when we are about to meet new people, or about to ride a rollercoaster and we've accidentally taken a load of ecstasy (it varies from person to person). But this is our mantra, this is how we live our lives: one tiny step at a time, one little 'we are OK' at a time.

For some of us anxiety, from its mildest form to its most complex iteration, is unavoidable and life-changing. The reasons for its origins in our think castles are various: environmental, sociological, genetic – but almost all of them are outside our control. At no point have we asked for this to be inflicted upon us, it is not our fault or our punishment, it is just the way the human brain adapts and protects itself. Some still think anxiety isn't a serious condition, that it's something that can be mocked and brushed aside. These things are simply not true. Anxiety's complexities are what causes so much damage, because even those of us who live with it on a daily basis still don't thoroughly understand it.

What I have attempted to provide with this book are simple ways to tackle your own anxiety, ways in which you can learn to understand it, and start to live like you again. We all deserve to live life the way we want, not in the 'I'm going to buy a small island with twenty greased-up men and build some sort of sex slide' way, but more in the way that we can get out of bed in the morning and, even if it is faking it, be a human person for a day. Life doesn't have to be a struggle, and the day-to-day doesn't have to feel laborious. Our brains are supposed to work for us and with us, not against us. As the news gets darker and darker on a daily basis, as life gets harder and the creeping thoughts of everything becoming a bit too much get closer, take a breath. As a society we often forget to take a breath and we simply react. Be it with an angry tweet, or a snide comment, or an irrational thought, we have become a species living on a planet where everything is going so fast, all the time, that we think we need to be fast too. That our judgements have to be fast, that our days have to be fast, when actually we need to just . . . breathe. As we learn to pre-empt our threats, to analyse our surroundings and start to look after ourselves properly, there is one thing to remember: the only human being on this absurd, confusing planet expecting something more from you, judging you, is you.

When threatened, the myotonic goat falls over. He stiffens his limbs and faints. It is, without a doubt, one of the most fucking ridiculous defence mechanisms in the animal kingdom. How easy is it to attack a goat that's fainted? The answer is, incredibly. The phrase 'Like shooting fish in a barrel' should be replaced with 'Like attacking a goat that's fainted'. However, it's one of the most relevant analogies in nature for anxiety. An over-arching sense of panic leads to a complete shutdown; it's a defence mechanism that has gone bananas, an evolutionary mishap that leaves the animal helpless. Don't be a fainting goat, be a platypus. Platypuses make no sense, the first person to ever find a platypus probably picked it up and screamed in horror: 'WHAT IS WRONG WITH THIS DOG?' But platypuses have endured – they are bizarre, but they have taken their evolutionary fuck-ups and gone, 'You know what, fuck it, I'm going with this.' It's not a perfect metaphor, but what I am trying to say is, take your evolutionary fuck-up, and own it.

Throughout the research for this book I asked the people I spoke to the question 'How would you define anxiety?' The question gets a different response from everyone you ask, and everyone has their own metaphor, but it all comes down to the same thing: you are constantly terrified of the future. Daisy defined it as 'being stuck in the present by a complete fear of the future'; Ruby described it as 'an infinity mirror: you see a problem and it multiplies and multiplies'; when I asked Mia her response was 'Some days it's simply a little niggle in the back of my mind that I can fight and be stronger than, other days it's a ten-foot brick wall around me in all directions with no windows.' My own definition would be 'the sudden feeling you get when you think you've forgotten your keys when you leave the house, but all the time and for no reason'. As a small practice, a little bit of homework if you will, I would like you to write your own definition of anxiety inside the front cover of this book. However you perceive it, however it affects you, your definition will be unique to you and, if you decide to pass the book on, will provide another insight into the condition.

It's getting near the end now I promise (of the book, not your life . . . and people say *I'm* depressing!) but I could go on trying to give you a self-confidence boost all day. I have no idea who you are, I have no idea how you are reading this, or if you are in fact planning on using this book as kindling or some sort of projectile to hunt squirrels. What I do know is that we can get through this; if your brain has the skills to generate anxiety, then it also has the tools and persistence to fight anxiety with both fists clenched and a proper escape route. Nothing is ever as bad as your brain tells you it is. There is always a way forward, a route with hope and a path that will be easier to walk than you could ever have predicted. It takes patience, it takes strength and it takes courage. You may feel like you simply do not have any of those qualities, but you do. They are there, they are just buried under piles of self-doubt, mountains of worry and, for some reason, heaps of song lyrics from the early 2000s that you probably shouldn't remember in such detail but you do anyway. A proper self-help book, written by a proper author with nice teeth and an even haircut, would tell you that it is potential that's hiding inside of you.

One morning you will get up, you'll look in the mirror with confidence, you'll shower and get dressed and then leave the house with the conviction of someone going to a free doughnuts and compliments convention. You'll speak with gravitas to people, you'll control your breathing with such ease that you'll win 'best human at breathing' at the international breathing awards four years in a row and you'll excel at what you put your mind to, because you and your mind are on even terms. After months, years, decades of living every day squabbling with the rambling nonsense box that is your brain, you won't even notice your brain as a separate entity. Life will be easier, being you will feel comfortable instead of a chore. You will not have cured your anxiety, but you will have come to an agreement with it. You will have trained it, you will be able to control it.

At the end of the day humans are all about self-preservation. We only have a short amount of time in this world and with that time we want to do as much as possible while at the same time not causing a fuss and not creating any grief for anyone else. That's what this book is about: self-preservation, regaining a sense of self, learning to look after your mind, realising that it is OK to worry about yourself. You aren't put on this planet and expected to be the best at everything, and to please everyone you meet; you are put on this planet to be the best version of you that you can possibly be. This sounds like such a simplistic idea, but, as we have learned, when you are dealing with the intricacies of the human brain, nothing is as easy as it sounds.

In the future, while anxiety still lives within you, it is no longer lurking in the shadows ready to jump out and thrust open its trench coat at you. It is now an active part of your psyche; it's a tool, a weapon you can use. We can turn what we now only know as fear into a tool to help us deal with the existential dread that is modern life. After all, our brain is just trying to protect us. Yes it's in bloody stupid ways like panic attacks and irrational worry, but – and I know that this is a revolutionary idea – let's take our evolutionary fuck-up and live with it, not let it define who we are. Let's use the tools anxiety has accidentally thrust upon us, a new sense of self, a new grounding in reality, a new sense of caution, empathy towards others, our concern for ourselves and other human beings. Let's help people, let's help ourselves. I know what you are thinking, and I agree: I *should* get the Nobel Peace prize for this completely original concept.

Life with anxiety doesn't have to be about bus milk, panic attacks and airport meltdowns, life with anxiety can be like having your own personal, if not entirely overactive, bodyguard. We developed anxiety to survive – and look, we're still here, so clearly it's done its job! But we've spent so much time surviving we forgot about the most important part of existence: actually enjoying ourselves while we're here. When you summon up the courage to look properly, you'll realise that the world isn't ending, so it's time to get out of survival mode, and start to live again.

IMPORTANT CONTACT NUMBERS

If you need any further information on mental health issues or anything else contained in the book, you can call any of the numbers listed here, or have a look at the websites.

⚡ Samaritans
   116 123 / www.samaritans.org
⚡ Mind
   0300 123 3393 / www.mind.org.uk
⚡ Campaign Against Living Miserably (CALM)
   0800 585 858 / www.thecalmzone.net
⚡ Anxiety UK
   0333 212 5820 / www.anxietyuk.org.uk
⚡ Time To Change
   www.time-to-change.org.uk
⚡ Off the Record (Bristol and south Gloucestershire)
   www.otrbristol.org.uk

ACKNOWLEDGEMENTS

This is the part where I thank people. The thing is, there are a lot of people to thank. I never thought I would be lucky enough to write a book, let alone a book about something so close to my heart, so please excuse me whilst I show my gratitude to some amazing people.

First, I'd like to thank Kate, Lisa, Alice, Emma and the whole Two Roads team for taking a chance on me and publishing this bag of nonsense; your support has been nothing short of amazing. Thanks to my agent Becky, who should be given an award for having to put up with me. Another thanks to my wife Lex, who has to be married to a bananas person and without whom this book wouldn't be possible. To my parents, Sharon and Iain: without them, I wouldn't be the person I am today, and their support throughout everything has been so amazing that putting it into words would do it a disservice. To my brother and my best friend Cal, thank you for being you and being the rational voice I needed when I couldn't find that voice myself. To Mia, Daisy, Dean and Ruby, who all shared their stories with me for no reason but to try and help others, which is the most amazing trait you can ever wish for. To my in-laws, Dave and Anne, who brought me various amounts of coffee as I researched and scribbled this book on their porch in the south of France. To my friends, Andy, Tom, Paul and Roly, who have been a constant source of encouragement and frankly just been some of the finest humans alive.

And most importantly I'd like to thank you, for reading this, because without you reading this, I'm just a weirdo throwing words at pages by himself. The one thing that has helped me through my battles with various mental health issues is the knowledge that I am not alone in this, and I hope this book can make you feel the same.